D1525609

UNDERSTANDING

JOHN IRVING

Understanding Contemporary American Literature

Matthew J. Bruccoli,
Editor

Bernard Malamud
by Jeffrey Helterman

James Dickey
by Ronald Baughman

John Hawkes
by Donald J. Greiner

Thomas Pynchon
by Robert D. Newman

Randall Jarrell
by J. A. Bryant, Jr.

Edward Albee
by Matthew C. Roudané

Contemporary American Drama
by William Herman

Vladimir Nabokov
by Stephen Jan Parker

Joyce Carol Oates
by Greg Johnson

Theodore Roethke
by Walter B. Kalaidjian

Mary Lee Settle
by George Garrett

Isaac Bashevis Singer
by Lawrence S. Friedman

George Garrett
by R. H. W. Dillard

Walker Percy
by Linda Whitney Hobson

Chicano Literature
by Carl R. Shirley
and Paula W. Shirley

Denise Levertov
by Harry Marten

Raymond Carver
by Arthur M. Saltzman

Katherine Anne Porter
by Darlene Harbour Unrue

Robert Bly
by William V. Davis

William Stafford
by Judith Kitchen

Carson McCullers
by Virginia Spencer Carr

John Barth
by Stan Fogel
and Gordon Slethaug

Ursula K. Le Guin
by Elizabeth Cummins

Contemporary American Science Fiction
by Thomas Clareson

Philip Roth
by Murray Baumgarten
and Barbara Gottfried

Kurt Vonnegut
by William Rodney Allen

Donald Barthelme
by Stanley Trachtenberg

Anne Tyler
by Alice Hall Petry

Joseph Heller
by Sanford Pinsker

William Kennedy
by J. K. Van Dover

John Irving
by Edward C. Reilly

Cynthia Ozick
by Lawrence S. Friedman

The Beats
by Edward Halsey Foster

E. L. Doctorow
by Douglas Fowler

Gary Snyder
by Patrick D. Murphy

UNDERSTANDING John IRVING

EDWARD C. REILLY

UNIVERSITY OF SOUTH CAROLINA PRESS

To My Children With Love
Heather Anne
Laurie Lynne
Erin Leigh
Jeffrey Sean
To Rags, Cathy Ivey, With Love,
And
To William Kennedy, In Admiration,
I Dedicate This Book

Second Printing 1992

Published in Columbia, South Carolina, by
the University of South Carolina Press

Manufactured in the United States of America

Library of Congress Cataloging-in-Publication Data

Reilly, Edward C.
Understanding John Irving / Edward C. Reilly.
p. cm. — (Understanding contemporary American literature)
Includes bibliographical references and index.
ISBN 0-87249-770-4 (hard cover)
ISBN 0-87249-880-8 (paperback)
1. Irving, John, 1942– —Criticism and interpretation.
I. Title. II. Series.
PS3559.R8Z85 1991
813′.54—dc20 91–14616

CONTENTS

Editor's Preface vi

Acknowledgments vii

Chapter 1 Understanding John Irving 1

Chapter 2 ''A Peculiar Novel'': *Setting Free the Bears* (1968) 15

Chapter 3 ''A Happy Ending . . . Absolutely Comic'': *The Water-Method Man* (1972) 33

Chapter 4 ''I Lost My Sense of Humor'': *The 158-Pound Marriage* (1974) 47

Chapter 5 ''The Best of the Four'': *The World According to Garp* (1976) 61

Chapter 6 ''The Most Complete Unto Itself'': *The Hotel New Hampshire* (1981) 81

Chapter 7 ''You Don't Compare Your Children'': *The Cider House Rules* (1985) 101

Chapter 8 ''The Magnitude of a Miracle'': *A Prayer for Owen Meany* (1989) 121

Bibliography 145

Index 153

EDITOR'S PREFACE

Understanding Contemporary American Literature has been planned as a series of guides or companions for students as well as good nonacademic readers. The editor and publisher perceive a need for these volumes because much of the influential contemporary literature makes special demands. Uninitiated readers encounter difficulty in approaching works that depart from the traditional forms and techniques of prose and poetry. Literature relies on conventions, but the conventions keep evolving; new writers form their own conventions—which in time may become familiar. Put simply, *UCAL* provides instruction in how to read certain contemporary writers—identifying and explicating their material, themes, use of language, point of view, structures, symbolism, and responses to experience.

The word *understanding* in the series title was deliberately chosen. Many willing readers lack an adequate understanding of how contemporary literature works; that is, what the author is attempting to express and the means by which it is conveyed. Although the criticism and analysis in the series have been aimed at a level of general accessibility, these introductory volumes are meant to be applied in conjunction with the works they cover. Thus they do not provide a substitute for the works and authors they introduce, but rather prepare the reader for more profitable literary experiences.

M. J. B.

ACKNOWLEDGMENTS

From *Setting Free the Bears* by John Irving. Copyright 1968 by John Irving. Reprinted by permission of Random House, Inc.

From *The Water-Method Man* by John Irving. Copyright 1972 by John Irving. Reprinted by permission of Random House, Inc.

From *The 158-Pound Marriage* by John Irving. Copyright 1974 by John Irving. Reprinted by permission of Random House, Inc.

From *The World According to Garp* by John Irving. Copyright 1976, 1977, 1978 by John Irving. Reprinted by permission of the publisher, Dutton, an imprint of New American Library, a division of Penguin Books USA Inc.

From *The Hotel New Hampshire* by John Irving. Copyright 1981 by Garp Enterprises, Ltd. Reprinted by permission of the publisher, Dutton, an imprint of New American Library, a division of Penguin Books USA Inc.

From *The Cider House Rules* by John Irving. Copyright 1985 by John Irving. Reprinted by permission of William Morrow & Company, Inc.

From *A Prayer for Owen Meany* by John Irving. Copyright 1989 by John Irving. Reprinted by permission of William Morrow & Company, Inc.

And with special thanks to Mary Ellen Mark/Library for providing the jacket photograph of Irving and to Teri Barbero, who coordinated the efforts for securing the photograph; to Carol Sue Johnson, who fortunately agreed to type another of my manuscripts and to keep my footnotes in proper sequence; to those who have graced my life: Sam Gennuso, Lyman Hagen, Jeff Watkins, Max

Dacus, Sr., and Bobbi, Cheryl, Jordan, and Christine Heskett; and especially to Cathy Ivey (AKA Rags), who, when I said, "Rags, read this chapter," or asked, "What do you think of this, Rags?" would proofread the copy, provide valuable suggestions, comments, occasional rages, and never miss a comma.

UNDERSTANDING
JOHN IRVING

CHAPTER ONE

Understanding John Irving

Career

John Winslow Irving was born on March 2, 1942, in Exeter, New Hampshire. His father, a World War II flyer, was shot down over Burma, survived the war, but Irving is not sure if he is still alive.[1] When Irving was six, his mother, Frances Winslow, married Colin F. N. Irving, a Russian history teacher at New Hampshire's Phillips Exeter Academy, and about whom Irving says: "I liked—loved—the man she married so well that I resented it when people referred to him as my stepfather. To do much prying might hurt their feelings: I thought that the past was none of my business. It was for me to imagine, not to ask."[2] Irving says that he had a "happy childhood" but an "uninteresting life."[3] He attended Phillips Exeter, where he was a "struggling C/B student" who required five years to graduate and where he became an aggressive wrestler and also decided to become a writer.

From 1961 to 1962 he attended the University of Pittsburgh because of its wrestling program, but he left when he "wasn't as good a wrestler as I had to be."[4] From

1963 to 1964, he attended the Institute of European Studies at the University of Vienna. Having fallen in love with Shyla Leary at Harvard, where he studied German before going to Vienna, he married her in Greece in 1964. He received his B.A. from the University of New Hampshire in 1965—the year his son Colin was born—and then completed his M.F.A. at the University of Iowa in 1967. In 1969, the Irvings moved to Vienna so he could work with movie director Irwin Kershner on an eventually aborted screen version of *Setting Free the Bears*; his son Brendan was born in 1970. In 1972 the Irvings returned to the United States and settled in Putney, Vermont. The Irvings were divorced in 1982, and in 1987, he married his second wife, Janet Turnbull, a literary agent whom he met in Toronto, Canada, where they still maintain an apartment in the Forrest Hill section.

Although *Setting Free the Bears* (1968) and *The Water-Method Man* (1972) sold over six thousand copies each, *The 158-Pound Marriage* (1974) only sold 2,560 copies.[5] Irving then switched from Random House to E. P. Dutton, a beneficial move for both author and publisher. Amid an advertising blitz, *The World According to Garp* sold 120,000 hardbound copies, and Irving received the critical acclaim that he deserved. *The Hotel New Hampshire* sold 150,000 copies, became a Book-of-the-Month-Club selection, and Pocket Books paid 2 million dollars for reprint rights. The film version of *Garp* premiered in 1982, and *The Hotel New Hampshire* film premiered in 1984. Financially solvent now, Irving did not have to teach and could henceforth devote himself to writing, and with *The Cider House Rules* and *A Prayer for Owen Meany*, his critical reputation continues to grow.

While denying that his works are strongly autobiographical, Irving admits that every writer uses "what little experience'' he may have, but he adds ''it's the translating, though, that makes the difference.''[6] Irving's novels do reflect what experiences he has had, and thus Exeter Academy is a model for Steering School in *Garp*; Vienna figures prominently in his first five novels; wrestling becomes a major metaphor in *The 158-Pound Marriage* and *Garp*; and his protagonists are either true orphans like Homer Wells or have lost at least one parent like Garp, the Berrys, and John Wheelwright. In the final analysis, however, Irving's mastery lies in his ability to transform these experiences through the art of his fiction to entertain and enlighten the reader about contemporary problems and life.

Overview

Except for *Setting Free the Bears*, his only novel with European settings and characters, John Irving's novels take place in twentieth-century United States, especially Maine and New Hampshire. Irving analyzes contemporary problems and issues plaguing his characters' lives. In addition, random violence and sudden death stalk his fictional worlds, a concept that has its inceptions in *Setting Free the Bears*.

Set primarily in Vienna, Austria, *Bears* traces Vienna's history from before the *Anschluss* (Austria's ''union'' with Nazi Germany in 1938) to after World War II. While admitting that *Bears* contains a ''large'' researched ''historical center''—''the Yugoslavian resistance in World War II, the Russian occupation of Vienna . . . the Nazi *Anschluss* of Austria in '38''—Irving claims that his succeeding novels do not have researched material as a ''central part of them. In the novel imagination wins out over research.''[7] For Irving, however, the violence, terror, and murders that preceded and followed the *Anschluss* not only established the precedent for World War II's brutal, chaotic fury, but also for the violence and bizarre deaths lurking in the postmodern world.

Vienna also becomes a secondary but important setting in *The Water-Method Man, The 158-Pound Marriage, The World According to Garp*, and *The Hotel New Hampshire*, novels in which his American characters, especially children, travel to Vienna as part of their maturing processes and the novels' bildungsroman motifs. Irving says, for example, "Growing up in a foreign country, you leave home in that sense. . . . And I attempt in writing . . . to use the experience of someone else's history, another country's history even, to make somebody painfully aware of his own meager grip on his or her surroundings."[8] Although Irving lived in Vienna during 1963 and 1964 and he and his family later lived in Vienna from 1969 to 1972, he emphasizes that Vienna is a "fairyland, really, more than a real place . . . a license to dream. And when I get there—when my characters journey there, or when they start there, or when they end up there—it's a place simply where 'something else' can happen."[9] His characters who experience Vienna, however, learn from its history so that they may better understand those forces shaping their lives, or as the narrator says about Garp's return to Vienna with his family, "The streets, the buildings, even the paintings in the museums, were like his old teachers, grown older."[10]

Although alluding to Wally Worthington's experiences in Burma when his plane is shot down during World War II, *The Cider House Rules* is the only novel in which the characters make no trips to a foreign country. In *A Prayer for Owen Meany*, Irving introduces another secondary but significant setting, Toronto, Canada, where Johnny Wheelwright reflects on the forces, especially the Vietnam War, that changed his and his friends' lives. While Vienna plays a violent role in twentieth-century history, Toronto is a tranquil no-man's-land; however, just as Vienna is the catalyst by which Irving assesses World War II's effects on his characters and their world, Toronto provides the basis for analyzing the Vietnam War's effects on the characters and the United States.

Whether in Vienna, Toronto, or the United States, Irving's settings underscore the violence and death that he sees at the core of life. Yet, in refuting critics who fault his plots for excessive violence, Irving asserts: "How could anyone who reads the newspaper think it excessive? I think events in American social and political life have borne me out. There have been more assassinations than exist in the novel, certainly more radical and terrorist groups. Perhaps I can be accused of having too sweet a disposition or being too optimistic, but not too violent or excessive."[11] Although the violence and death within his plots may emphasize "how perilous and fragile our lives can be,"[12] Irving maintains that his literary vision is affirmative, a point emphasized in his wry comment about *Garp*: "I've written a life-affirming novel in which everybody dies."[13] "There are no happy endings," Irving says, but "that's no cause for some blanket cynicism or sophomoric despair. That's just a strong incentive to live purposefully, to be determined about living well."[14] This maxim often governs his characters' lives, especially the Berry family in *Hotel New Hampshire*.

Irving praises Charles Dickens, John Cheever, and Kurt Vonnegut, who all write about their characters with "grace and affection."[15] Grace and affection certainly apply to the way Irving writes about his characters. Critics label Irving's characters zany, wacky, or eccentric, yet in their determination to live well and purposefully, their fears, follies, vanities, and virtues are recognizably human. While admitting that he did not especially admire Siggy or Hannes in *Bears*, Bogus Trumper in *Water-Method Man*, or the narrator in *158-Pound Marriage*, Irving "admired and cared for" the *Garp* characters, an admiration certainly extending to his succeeding characters.

In developing his characters, Irving subjects them to extreme situations—"sexual situations or violent ones or whatever"—to bring out the "best and the worst aspects of ourselves . . . the things we admire or despise about people":

> Basically I always try to place my characters under the most and least favorable circumstances to see how they will react, to test them. In *Garp* this strategy was very self-conscious: I wanted to create characters whom I greatly admired and then bless them with incredibly good fortune in the first half of the novel. . . . But in the second half of the novel, I visit all the worst kinds of extreme things on these people to see how they would deal with extremes of adversity, just as earlier they had to cope with success.[16]

This emotional-extremes technique is most effective in Irving's bildungsroman motifs as children like T. S. Garp, the Berrys, Homer Wells, Johnny Wheelwright, and Owen Meany learn and mature from their experiences with life's extremes. For example, his child characters usually lose either one or both parents. Siggy Javotnik's father, Utch's parents, and Garp's father are World War II victims; the Berrys' mother dies in a plane crash; Homer Wells never knew his father or mother; and a foul ball kills Wheelwright's mother. The bildungsroman motif not only develops these characters' rites-of-passage but also complements the novels' actions, settings, and themes—for example, Garp and the Berrys travel to Vienna to learn more about life, death, love, and happiness.

How his characters live happy, meaningful lives varies from novel to novel, but the bases for their happiness remain constant: accepting responsibility; appreciating life's beauties and gifts; refusing to be intimidated by life's nebulous forces; and especially loving friends and family. The family unit, in fact, becomes the "defense against the abyss" of the contemporary world, and Irving says he "could not state a better or broader opinion of family life" than in *Garp*.[17] Moreover, in refuting critics who fault him for the bizarre forces plaguing his fictional families, Irving retorts:

> But let's take a simple family of four. Those two children will have, say, two children, making eight people. Is it claiming too much that out of the eight, someone is going to hit the wall? In a car crash, a plane crash, a wipeout, a premature tragedy, of course, it will happen! Someone is going off the deep end. They may not jump out a window, they may take drugs until they are useless, but certainly one of those eight isn't going to make it.[18]

To complement the plot twists that carry his characters from fortune to misfortune, Irving juxtaposes the tragic with the comic. The tragic-comic extremes also drive his characters to the edge and determine their worth or worthlessness. Regarding life, Irving declares: "When people are happy—when we're in love, when we have orgasms of one kind or another, when we're proud of our children or high on ourselves—it strikes me that we are happy indeed. And who can say the world isn't comic, especially at those times? But we have pain too. Quite simply, the pain wins."[19] As the narrator in *Garp* says, "an evening could be hilarious and the next morning murderous" (406).

Despite the pain and tragedy, Irving's novels end affirmatively because his characters have meaningful, happy lives. Indeed, Irving's affirmative vision is evident in some of his concluding chapter titles: "Congratulations to All You Survivors" (*Bears*); "The Old Friends Assemble For Throgsgafen Day" (*Water-Method Man*); "Life After Garp" (*Garp*). His other novels conclude with affirmative images and sentences: "You've got to get obsessed and stay obsessed. You have to keep passing the open windows" (*Hotel New Hampshire*); "there was no fault to be found in the hearts of either Dr. Stone or Dr. Larch who were—if there ever were—Princes of Maine, Kings of New England" (*Cider House*); "they were the forces we didn't have the faith to feel, they were the forces we failed to believe in. . . . Oh God, please give him back" (*Owen Meany*).

Among Irving's other literary techniques are refrains that Irving defines as those "little litanies . . . that serve to mark how far you've come, and also forewarn you about where you're going. . . . In *The Hotel New Hampshire* there are several refrains: Sorrow floats, keep passing the open windows, everything as a fairy tale."[20] Other such verbal refrains would include the "gale of the world" (*Bears*); the "whole thing" (*158-Pound Mar-*

riage); the "rules" and "wait and see" (*Cider House*); the "voice" and the "dream" (*Owen Meany*). Refrains also comprise actions—riding motorcycles (*Bears*); writing a dissertation (*Water-Method Man*); weight lifting (*Hotel New Hampshire*); reading from *David Copperfield*, *Great Expectations*, and *Jane Eyre* (*Cider House*); or slam-dunking basketballs (*Owen Meany*). Although critics often interpret these refrains as needless repetition, they form the plot threads that augment settings, characterizations, conflicts, and themes; they also illuminate Irving's intricate plotting techniques.

In addition to refrains, Irving's metaphors highlight the novels' themes. While World War II, a clogged urinary tract, writing, and cities may be metaphors, Irving's sport metaphors typify their functions: "To use one of my wrestling metaphors," says Irving, "if you're going to prepare yourself mentally and physically for a tough match on the weekend, the best way to do it is to get the shit kicked out of you by one of your teammates on Tuesday or Wednesday. If you work with something that is brutal and demanding, day-by-day, you'll be better equipped to deal with the real traumas later on."[21] In this sense, wrestling prepares Garp for his writing career; weight lifting gives John Berry the strength to protect his family by squeezing the life out of Arbeiter, a German terrorist; and slam-dunking basketballs enables Meany to consummate his life's quest. Moreover, because of the grueling discipline required for both sports, Garp and John Berry can deal with the personal traumas haunting their lives, and Meany can accept his ultimate fate.

Symbols also underscore the novels' meanings, and Irving believes that symbols should always be clear: "There's not much point in symbols if people don't understand them. If you're going to be symbolic, you'd better let people know you are.''[22] Irving's symbols range from wrestling rooms, hotels, a foul ball, an armadillo, bears, to the Under Toad and the Berrys' Labrador retriever, Sorrow. The Under Toad and Sorrow symbolize life's overwhelming forces—e.g., terror, violence, and death. In contrast, in *Bears* and *Hotel New Hampshire* bears suggest the characters' bearish tenacity to survive when confronting those forces. As do refrains, Irving's symbols acquire depth and meaning as the plots develop and thus highlight his intricate plotting techniques.

Irving's are action-filled, expansive novels, facts attributable to his appreciation of and love for nineteenth-century fiction. In addition to Turgenev, Tolstoi, and Dostoevsky, he admires Thomas Hardy and especially Charles Dickens, whom he still reads for pleasure. ''I was raised,'' says Irving, ''on European novels, particularly British nineteenth century; I like character and storytelling; I like plot.''[23] Irving also appreciates Joseph Conrad, Virginia Woolf, and John Hawkes. Irving even refers to his works as ''big novels'' since they trace ''somebody's life in its *entirety* . . . I mean to move characters through time, so we can see how they've changed—in their lives and by their lives. I think the novel that interests me now is a novel that shows us how people *end up*. I feel I am programmed to write big novels, or at least long ones.''[24]

Because he admired the nineteenth-century novels, especially Dickens, Irving is fond of epilogues. ''I begin with an ending, or an idea of an ending. I begin with a sense of an epilogue, and in that way there is at least an objective ahead of you.''[25] While his epilogues recount events and lives after the novel's official close—e.g., the ''Life After Garp'' section—Irving's epilogues are necessary for his "big novels": "I knew a novel that did not convey the passage and perspective of time did not interest me. I wanted to write about the passing of and perspective of time and the softening of pain. An epilogue inevitably has nostalgia in it—it's a way of saying, 'It's not so bad what happened to that little child.' No one has a 'happy ending.' 'Ending' is by definition not a happy occurrence."[26]

Irving's novels may be about prep school life, writers' lives, wrestling, Vienna, and Toronto, all experiences common to Irving's life, but he adamantly claims that his novels are not solely autobiographical, "I honestly don't think I could have eked out even one novel from the experiences in my own life."[27] He does concede, however, that while he may use autobiography as a "stepping-off point in fiction . . . something to use up and get over,"[28] translating these experiences into fiction comprises the art. "I don't even feel obligated in my fiction to tell the truth. The truth of what's happened to me is mostly irrelevant to what I write about."[29]

Because he focuses on contemporary issues that include homosexuality, transvestism, mate-swapping, equal rights, radical extremism, incest, rape, abortion, and violence, some critics label Irving a "trendy" or "popular" writer; because of his probing insights into and analyses of these issues, other critics label him a "serious" writer. Although in conceding that he writes sentences and paragraphs that keep the reader interested, Irving claims that these "openly seductive" elements are not aspects of "commercialism but part of the writer's responsibility":

> Art has an aesthetic responsibility to be entertaining. The writer's responsibility is to take the hard stuff and

> make it as accessible as the stuff can be made. Art and entertainment aren't contradictions. It's only been in the last decade, or last twenty years, that there has somehow developed this rubric under which art is expected to be difficult. . . . By creating a taste for literature that needs interpretation, we, of course, create jobs for reviewers, for critics, for the academy. I like books that can be read without those middlemen.[30]

While Irving's subject matter may be the "stuff" of popular fiction, his analyses of and insights into these contemporary problems are the "stuff" of serious fiction. R. Z. Sheppard establishes Irving's place in contemporary American fiction: "In the 50s J. D. Salinger produced *Catcher in the Rye*, the *Huckleberry Finn* of the Silent Generation. Readers in the 60s and early 70s rallied around Kurt Vonnegut's *Cat's Cradle* with its 'karass,' and the casually philosophical 'so it goes' from *Slaughterhouse Five*. The end of the decade belongs to Irving and Garpomania."[31] *The World According to Garp* provided Irving the critical accolades he deserved, and *The Hotel New Hampshire*, *The Cider House Rules*, and *A Prayer for Owen Meany* have further enhanced John Irving's critical reputation as an "accessible" serious writer.

NOTES

1. Corby Kummer, "John Irving: Fascinated by Orphans." In a letter dated 22 June 1990, Heather Cochran, assistant to John Irving, wrote, "As for the name of Mr. Irving's father, he regrets that he is unable to provide that information for you."
2. *Ibid.*
3. Gabriel Miller, *John Irving*, 1.
4. Greil Marcus, "John Irving: The World of *The World According to Garp*," 70.

5. Scott Haller, "John Irving's Bizarre World," 32.

6. Marcus, "The World of *The World According to Garp*," 71. See also Edward C. Reilly, "Life Into Art: Some Notes on Irving's Fiction."

7. Joyce Renwick, "John Irving: An Interview," 15.

8. Miller, *John Irving*, 181.

9. Renwick, "Interview," 15.

10. John Irving, *The World According to Garp*, 341.

11. Richard West, "John Irving's World After *Garp*," 32.

12. Larry McCaffery, "An Interview with John Irving," 3.

13. Renwick, "Interview," 10.

14. Thomas Williams, "Talk with John Irving," *New York Times Book Review*, 23 April 1978, 6. These words also become the Berry family's maxims in Chapter Six of *Hotel New Hampshire*.

15. McCaffery, "Interview," 18.

16. *Ibid.*, 14–15.

17. Renwick, "Interview," 13.

18. West, "Irving's World After *Garp*," 32.

19. Williams, "Talk with John Irving," 26.

20. Laura de Coppet, "An Interview with John Irving," 44.

21. McCaffery, "Interview," 14.

22. de Coppet, "Interview," 44.

23. *Ibid.*, 42.

24. Renwick, "Interview," 6.

25. *Ibid.*

26. Barbara Bannon, "*PW* Interviews John Irving," 6.

27. McCaffery, "Interview," 3.

28. *Ibid.*

29. *Ibid.*

30. *Ibid.*, 10–11.

31. R. Z. Sheppard, "Life into Art: Garp Creator John Irving Strikes Again," 46.

CHAPTER TWO

"A Peculiar Novel": *Setting Free the Bears* (1968)

John Irving began writing *Setting Free the Bears* while enrolled in the Writers' Workshop at the University of Iowa. Although Irving calls *Bears* "a peculiar novel," he says the novel that "meant the most" to him before and "all during the time" he worked on *Bears* was *The Tin Drum* by Günter Grass, whom Irving praises for Grass's "extraordinary" imagination and "narrative momentum"[1]—qualities certainly evident in *Bears* and Irving's later fiction. *Bears* sold 6,228 copies,[2] and, while not as uniformly excellent as his later works, it provides a Baedeker to Irving's other novels in its setting, characters, themes, and narrative techniques.

Bears is divided into three sections. "Part One: Siggy" takes place in 1967 and focuses upon Siegfried "Siggy" Javotnik and Hannes Graff, the picaresque protagonists, who drop out of the University of Vienna, purchase an old 700cc British Royal Enfield motorcycle, and tour Austria. During their odyssey, Siggy decides that they should free the animals in Vienna's Heitzinger Zoo. "Part Two: The Notebook" has a dual focus. In the "Zoo Watch" section, Siggy clandestinely reconnoiters the zoo to formulate plans for the zoo bust. Interspersed among the zoo watches is "The Highly Selective Autobiography of Siegfried Javotnik" that details both the history of Siggy's family and Vienna from 1935 to the Nazi *Anschluss* and through World War II and the Russian occupation. "Part Three: Setting Them Free" concerns Hannes Graff's efforts to free the animals once Siggy is killed in a bizarre motorcycle crash.

Although secondary settings include Yugoslavia and the Austrian countryside, the novel's primary setting is Vienna before, during, and after World War II. As recounted in Siggy's "Selective Autobiography," the Nazi *Anschluss* becomes the vortex into which swirl the fates of Vienna and Siggy's grandparents and parents. After beginning on May 30, 1935, as Zahn Glanz courts Hilke Marter, Siggy's mother-to-be, the next entry shifts quickly to February 22, 1938, when Vienna's fate becomes fixed, sealed, and foreshadowed by an escalation of terror and violence. Otto Planetta, for instance, boldly assassinates Engleburt Dolfuss, Chancellor of Austria, and through political machinations and intimidations, the Nazis seize control of the Austrian Cabinet, an usurpation so rapid that Glanz remarks, "Just ten days now and we've got five Nazis on the Cabinet," to which another character wryly replies, "Half a Nazi a day."[3] As Nazi control escalates, so do the terrorist actions of reported "look-alike gangs of youths" who sprawl their legs in tramway and theater aisles, who harass young women, and who, marching "arm in arm" and sometimes "in step," shoulder people off sidewalks. Irving symbolizes the impending violence accompanying the *Anschluss* in an incident in which Zahn and Hilke see a brutalized yet live squirrel jumping, spinning, and reeling in circles with a "pink and perfect, hairless swastika carved on its head" (111), an image prefiguring the serial numbers tattooed on Nazi death-camp inmates.

The violence escalates even more as a "look-alike gang" chases an old Jew who slips on icy trolley tracks and dies under a trolley's wheels. According to Klag Brahms, a witness, either the old Jew "was running very fast, or was caught in a gale" (117). Later, the violence becomes even more grotesquely inhumane when Radio Johannesgasse reports Mara Madoff's murder, her body "found hanging in her coat on a coat hook in the second balcony wardrobe closet of the Vienna State Opera House" (122). The report impassively continues:

> Authorities attribute the cause of her death to a star-shaped series of fine-pointed stab wounds in the heart. . . . The authorities say that the young woman was in no way assaulted; however, her stockings were missing and her shoes had been put back on. Late last night someone claims to have seen a group of young men at Haroff Keller; allegedly, one of them wore a pair of women's stockings for a scarf. But among the young men, these days, this is a common way of showing off. (122)

The official, impersonal language of this report suggests the similar lack of concern about the political machinations that topple the Austrian government and facilitate the *Anschluss*. Moreover, when the Nazis invade Austria on Black Friday, March 11, 1938, Siggy's autobiography notes that the "first wave of Gestapo arrests took seventy-six thousand" (156), a statement underscoring the ultimate escalation of violence.

Siggy's autobiography also records the Russian occupation's effects on Vienna. Similar to the *Anschluss*'s terrors, the Russian occupation results in mass arrests, beatings, rapes, and murders. A patrolling Russian soldier accidentally machine-guns Siggy's grandmother when she joyously opens the apartment window to announce the news of Siggy's birth. In an incident reminiscent of Mara Madoff's murder, Anna Hellein, a young Viennese social worker, is dragged from her train by a Soviet guard, raped, murdered, left on the rails, and decapitated by the next train. Moreover, the Allied Council's refusal to investigate either Grandmother Marter's death, Hellein's murder, or the other "eleven recent murders by men in Soviet uniform" suggests an unconscionable lack of concern similar to that which precipitated the *Anschluss*. The Benno Blum gang, Black Market traffickers, also typifies the Russian occupation. The Blum gang deftly murders people—official reports merely list them as "disappeared"—and then skulk back to the Russian sector and asylum, even though the Russians claim they too are hunting the gang members. While the Benno Blum gang recalls the "look-alike" gangs that terrorized Vienna before the *Anschluss*, the Blum gang also prefigures the terrorists and radical extremists that eminently figure in Irving's later novels.

In *Bears*, Vienna symbolizes, therefore, the old world and its values, traditions, and culture that will inexorably plunge toward chaos and violence. Chancellor Kurt Von Schuschnigg's "backward" steps before Adolf Hitler's relentless ultimatums represent a retreat into chaos, or as Schuschnigg predicts in his study entitled *Austrian Requiem*: "And now all is over. Humanity holds its breath, the old world with the new, perhaps for the first time in history. . . . Some of it can never be repaired."[4] Mara Madoff's murder in the Vienna State Opera House during a production of Wagner's *Lohengrin* depicts another backward step toward violence and chaos. The opera house symbolizes refinement and culture, and *Lohengrin*, the opera about an early German knight who rescues a maiden and wins her love, contrasts with Madoff's brutal murder by a symbol of the new German hero, a youthful Nazi thug. As another concentric circle spreading outward from the *Anschluss* and the war, the Russian occupation extends the violence and chaos in Vienna. According to Gabriel Miller, "Irving's preoccupation with Vienna and the *Anschluss* is significant because it is based on a recognition that this was the beginning of the horror that was to become the post-modern world, the forerunner of the escalation to the Holocaust, Hiroshima, and the Cold War."[5] Because they have been shaped by it, Siggy and Graff must understand Vienna's history, and Siggy writes that Vienna is "all pre-history—smug and secretive. . . . But if we're supposed to be the generation that's to profit from our elder's mistakes, I feel I ought to know everyone's error" (107). Similarly, in the later novels, Irving's American characters will travel to and learn from their experiences in postwar Vienna.

As a secondary but significant setting, Yugoslavia suggests escalating terror and chaos on a greater, more dehumanizing scale. For example, Colonel Drazha Mihailovich's Chetniks, Jospip Broz Tito's Communist partisans, and Ante Pavelich's pro-Croatian terrorists wage a brutal, chaotic war in Yugoslavia that is symbolized by a scene in which Javotnik and Gottlob Wut see a raft piled with Serbian heads after an Ustashi victory:

> The raft was neatly piled with heads; the architect had attempted a pyramid. It was almost perfect. But one head near the peak had slipped out of place; its hair

> was caught between other heads, and it swung from face to face in the river wind; some faces watched the swinging, and some looked away. (198)

Appropriately, the raft's macabre cargo suggests the civil war's and World War II's fury as well as the helpless fates of people who are caught up in the fury that they can neither understand nor control.

Colonel Drazha Mihailovich's execution typifies Yugoslavia's internecine chaos of "too many side wars." He successfully leads the Chetniks against the Nazis, is promoted to general, but is eventually hunted, captured, and executed by Tito's Communists; or, as Bijelo Slivnica says: "The Chetniks fight the Germans, the partisans fight the Germans, and in a little while the whole Red Army will be here—fighting Germans. In between Germans and after Germans, partisans and the Red Army will fight Chetniks—claiming that Chetniks side with the Germans. Good propaganda is what counts" (187–88). Siggy emphasizes the chaos when he writes, "There were too many side wars within the war; whole sides were changing sides" (187). At his trial Mihailovich says, "I wanted much . . . I started much . . . but the gale of the world blew away me and my work" (261). The emphasis on the "gale of the world" not only highlights Mihailovich's helplessness before life's overwhelming forces (e.g., "good propaganda") but also recalls the head swinging in the river wind and the old Jew, who "caught in a gale," dies under the trolley's wheels. Moreover, Mihailovich's eventual abandonment by the Yugoslavians—"He was abandoned" cries Javotnik (233)—not only mirrors the Austrian government's abandonment of social and moral principles but also recalls the scene in the latrine when

Javotnik abandons Gottlob Wut. As a secondary setting, Yugoslavia depicts, therefore, another concentric circle spreading outward from the *Anschluss* to include the chaotic, brutal fury of the Yugoslavian civil wars and World War II.

All of the characters are uprooted by the war and thus their lives become chaotic. Siggy records, for instance, that Gottlob Wut has been "uprooted by the war, which isn't a thing you could say for all Germans" (165); that Wut does not "seem to give a damn for the whole war" (167); and that when he finally deserts, he only wants to "devote his time to motorcycles, not to escape anything in particular" (199). The Marters' uprootedness is evident in their moving back and forth from Vienna and Kaprun, and Javotnik travels constantly to escape the war. Siggy and Hannes have also been uprooted by the war—Siggy when his family moves to Kaprun and Graff when his family moves to a neutral country. Siggy and Graff are, to quote Siggy, in "an interim age in an interim time . . . a womb and a pre-womb existence at a time when great popular decisions with terrible consequences were being made" (106).

Regarding his protagonists, Irving admits, "I did not admire Siggy or Graff . . . I knew them, knew what they were like, and I could tell you about them."[6] Although not as well developed as Irving's later characters, Siggy and Graff epitomize the 1960s anti-heroes, and a prefatory editor's blurb in *Bears* refers to them as "merry pranksters," a term recalling Ken Kesey's Merry Pranksters. Furthermore, Siggy's and Graff's motorcycle odyssey and quest to live off the land and to free the zoo animals coincide with the free-spirit movements of the 1960s and 1970s.

In terms of moving through experiences to knowledge, Siggy learns from his family's ordeals, but because Siggy dies in the first section, Graff's rites of passage become the novel's final thrust. Graff must deal with the failure of Siggy's ideal plans once the zoo bust plummets from chaos into carnage. The primates, for example, demolish the zoo's *Biergarten* in a "vandalism of a shocking human nature" (320), a destruction compounded when the African elephant tramples bushes and flattens iron rails. The destruction turns to carnage when the "big cats" devour other animals and especially when the townspeople slaughter the animals with pitchforks, sledgehammers, fireplace tridents, and guns. The escalating chaos and death during the zoo bust recall the escalating violence in Vienna before, during, and after the *Anschluss* and World War II.

The zoo fiasco also results in Graff's nadir when he is "rendered inert" and realizes that perhaps the animals would have fared better had he not "meddled in the unsatisfactory scheme of things" (332). As typical with Irving's later protagonists, however, Graff's bleakest moment becomes enlightening, especially when the Rare Spectacled Bears huff out of the forest. Thankful that their escape did not assume the "custardlike quality of too many other endings"—e.g., the novel's other bizarre deaths and especially Javotnik's—Graff understands that to survive he must accept responsibility for his actions and battle life's overwhelming forces, e.g., the "unsatisfactory scheme of things." As the novel ends, he is no longer inert, so he rides the Royal Enfield out of the ditch (his nadir), onto the road (life's flow), and into the "full-force wind" (life's forces). "Properly balanced" and "steady" (his physical and mental states), Graff exults, "I truly outdrove the wind. For sure, for the moment, at least—there was no gale hurrying me out of the world'' (335). Determined to live meaningfully and learn from experiences, Graff will now visit Ernst Watzek-Trummer whom he describes as, ''Historian without equal, and keeper of details. He should make a fine confessor for me'' (335). As implied in the chapter's title, ''Congratulations to All You Survivors,'' Graff survives; furthermore, the last chapter typifies Irving's epilogues that assuage the tragic pains and emphasize his affirmative vision.

For that matter, Ernst-Watzek-Trummer also survives far more dangerous situations than Graff, namely the *Anschluss*, World War II, the Russian occupation, and the tragic deaths of the Marters, his adopted family. Ernst survives because he learns from history and life. He reads voraciously and often puts aside new books because he says, ''I know it already'' (252); furthermore, he discusses politics, world affairs, and the Marter's history with Javotnik and Grandfather. Finally, as a survivor, Ernst becomes responsible and compassionate, two key Irvingesque virtues. Not only does Ernst accept his ''burial responsibilities . . . for two generations of deaths in the Marter family,'' but Siggy notes: ''Ernst Watzek-Trummer. Keeper of the family album—egg man, postman, historian, survivor. Responsible, finally, for seeing I would survive to understand my heritage'' (263, 245).

As a Baedeker to Irving's other novels, *Bears* emphasizes, however, that survival is often temporary. The Marters survive by moving from Vienna to Kaprun, but still death intervenes. Vratno Javotnik masters various languages and aliases to escape the war's fury only to be murdered by Todor Slivnica. Gottlob Wut deserts only to be murdered by members of his Motorcycle Unit

Balkan 4. Grandfather Marter, Draza Mihailovich, and even Siggy epitomize temporary survivals in a chaotic world. Though Ernst and Graff survive, Graff's "for the moment, at least" suggests temporary survivals, an idea later echoed in *Garp*'s concluding sentence, "In the world according to Garp, we are all terminal cases" (437).

Setting Free the Bears contains other Irvingesque themes, some of which, such as rape, become more significant and developed in later novels. For example, in *Bears*, rapes are peripheral actions that happen to Mara Madoff and Anna Hellein and thus underscore the general theme of violence; however, in *Garp*, *Hotel New Hampshire*, and *Cider House*, rape directly affects the major characters' families and lives. In addition, whereas the Slivnica family represents brutality and selfish profiteering, the Hilke family unit provides a bulwark against chaos and violence, but unlike the stronger family units in the later novels, the Hilke family disintegrates as its members die. Finally, in *Bears*, violent deaths stalk both primary and secondary characters. Siggy is stung to death when he crashes his motorcycle into a farm wagon loaded with bee hives; Gottlob Wut is stuffed headfirst down a "stand-up crapper stall" (210) to suffocate; Todor Slivnica pulverizes Vratno Javotnik like custard; Hilke returns to Vienna and is never heard from again; Grandfather Marter rides the mail sled to his death down the Suicide Trail ski slope.

As in Irving's later novels, *Bears* has refrains that either through action or verbal repetitions underscore plot techniques. As an instance of action refrains, Siggy frees Frau Ertl's goats, they refuse to bolt, and the town's children easily recapture them, lighter actions foreshadowing the chaotic zoo bust when the townspeople slaughter the animals. Although Javotnik's and Wut's motorcycle odyssey is potentially more precarious, Siggy's and Graff's motorcycle trips loosely parallel the former because the purpose of both journeys is escape and freedom. Buried headfirst so that only his soles protrude from the mulch, Borsa Durd's death will be reflected in Wut's headfirst death down the latrine stall. A Viennese man is accidentally machine-gunned for urinating out his window, and Frau Marter is machine-gunned for yelling out her window. Moreover, the chaotic, absurd "gale of the world" that blows Mihailovich away is mirrored in the old Jew who, as if caught in a "gale," dies under tramway wheels and in the Russian officer who is blown down the street by the machine-gunner who killed Frau Marter. Even Siggy's death is a variation of the "gale of the world," or as Graff says, "It was no gale of the world that got you, Sig. You made your own breeze, and it blew you away" (261). The "gale of the world" metaphor not only applies to the novel's other numerous deaths, but the metaphor also resurfaces in the guise of the Under Toad in *Garp* and Sorrow in *Hotel New Hampshire*.

One of the novel's symbols is bears, a symbol reappearing in *Garp* and *Hotel New Hampshire*. Among Irving's bear symbolisms, the Asiatic Black Bear in *Bears* is the darkest symbol. Described as "particularly ferocious," the Black Bear becomes "enraged" when he sees other animals, and so his cage faces away from the other cages. The Black Bear is also described as being "unfamiliar with compromise" and as standing "like an assassin in his cage" (307, 321). Once he is freed during the zoo bust, the Black Bear's roar causes "hysteria" among the other animals, none of which wants his "unreasonable company" (323, 324). In addition, Hannes Graff realizes that the zoo animals, are "all different. . . . Just like people" and concludes that in the "Hietzinger Playhouse with everyone playing his own separate role, of not living together, . . . there are just three choices: the anticlimax; no climax at all; or the raging, unreasonable but definite climax demanded by the Famous Asiatic Black Bear" (307, 311). With its uncompromising ferociousness, assassin's stance, and raging climax, the Black Bear symbolizes the ultimate brutality of those gale-of-the-world forces at the novel's core: Hitler's uncompromising ultimatums to Chancellor Schuschnigg; the Nazi violence before, during, and after the *Anschluss*; the chaotic Yugoslavian civil war; the terror during the Russian occupation; and the numerous bizarre deaths stalking the characters' lives.

In contrast, with "cartoon" countenances as if they had been "laughed right out of Ecuador" (18), the pair of Rare Spectacled Bears symbolize cooperation, hope, and survival. Before the zoo bust as Graff and Gallen argue, Graff says that the Spectacled Bears sigh as if implying, "Oh, don't fight among each other. . . . Never fight among each other. In close quarters, it's not wise. You'll find there's no one else" (306). In contrast with the Asiatic Black Bear that is caged alone and "not familiar with compromise," the Spectacled Bears, when freed, lope "shoulder to shoulder . . . butting themselves into umbrellas and hissing monkeys" (307, 320–21). This cooperation underscores the lack of cooperation—the fighting "in close quarters"—evident in the Austrian Cabinet and in the Yugoslavian civil wars. Because they run "shoulder to shoulder" and butt paths through the destruction and other animals, they survive the carnage. In addition, the Spectacled Bears' steady pace—"not an unreasonable speed''—and their ''inexhaustible'' energy and determination to run ''back to the Andes . . . Or at least the Alps'' provide hope and clues for Graff's survival and suggest why he is steady, balanced, and determined as he rides into the ''full-force wind'' (333, 335), and perhaps an extenuation of the ''gale of the world'' refrain.

Bears also juxtaposes comedy with tragedy. Ernest Watzek-Trummer, for example, fashions an Austrian Eagle costume from tin pie plates and chicken feathers. Although his intent is patriotic and serious, he is ordered from trolleys and taunted by children because of his ridiculous costume. However, when he arrives at the Augustiner Keller and caws, ''Austria is free,'' Grandfather Marter treats this patriotic symbol with the utmost dignity and respect, and the other drinkers ''rush to embrace the national symbol'' (128). When Zahn Glanz dons the eagle suit the next day and drives his taxi through Vienna, a comedy that could be from the Keystone Cops results. An early churchgoer rolls out of the taxi when he sees the costume, limps to the curb, and rants about seeing an angel. Laundress Drexa Neff swears that some inhuman creature has attacked her and kneels on the sidewalk—''fanny up, she seems to be expecting some ungentlemanly visit from a god'' (140). In an attempt to capture Zahn, now called ''the birdman,'' a street worker bravely jumps on the taxi's running board, and Zahn opens the door, but, rather than be dashed against the Academy of Graphic Arts' archway, the worker lets go in another Keystone-Cops scenario: ''In his rearview mirror, he can see the worker back-pedaling and almost catching up with his own momentum. But he topples over a little foolishly, and somersaults out of Zahn's mirror'' (138). These pell-mell, comic scenes underscore the tragic horror unfolding as the Austrian government collapses foolishly around Schuschnigg, who is tragically back-pedaling, as the Nazi terror escalates and the *Anschluss* becomes more imminent. Thus Ernst's and Zahn's patriotic but comic romps through Vienna sadly celebrate what Grandfather Marter realizes is "Austria's last fling" (130).

Todor Slivnica's characterization combines humor and horror, but whereas the eagle-suit scenes are comic, Todor's ghastly sense of humor emphasizes his passively vicious personality. Regarding his retarded, twin sisters, Baba and Julka, he says, "They share one brain between them. It's a small allowance to live on," to which Bijelo Slivnica replies, "Enough humor, Todor" (164). When he learns that Vratno Javotnik is a linguist, Todor wonders what language Vratno would speak with "glass dust in his larynx," and again Bijelo cautions, "That's enough humor, Todor" (164). When describing Vratno's fate, Todor seizes some custard in one huge fist, smashes the custard with his other fist, and sardonically replies, "Where is Vratno Javotnik? Why he's here, on your nose, and here, on the lantern overhead—and even here! In space," to which Siggy adds: "Todor, among other things, was known for his sense of humor" (238). Such grim humor recalls other scenes: when one of the Nazi toughs shows off and wears Mara Madoff's stockings as a scarf; when Wut is suffocated in a latrine stall; when the "architect" attempts a "pyramid" of heads on the raft. Although some people like Bijelo or the Nazi thugs may think these incidents are humorous, they represent sinister, impassive forces that snuff out lives and thus underscore the actual terror and tragedies inherent in the plot.

Finally, *Bears* contains a narrative within a narrative. The road-novel and rites-of-passage motifs frame the secondary plots, the zoo watches, and Siggy's autobiography. In addition, just as the zoo bust progresses toward chaos and carnage, so does Siggy's autobiography as it moves from the *Anschluss* and World War II to the Cold War. Occurring in 1967 as does the main plot, the zoo watch sections look backward and forward in time to complement both the main plot and Siggy's autobiography. O. Schrutt, the zoo's diabolical night watchman, for example, parodies the Nazis' brutality since he terrorizes the animals with a truncheon and an electric prod just as he progressed from one of the Hitler Youths to a Nazi soldier who terrorized the Jews. As Graff stuns Schrutt with the electric prod, threatens to shoot his elbows off, and leads him to an appropriate cage, these actions suggest how the Nazis treated the Jews.

Similarly, just as the main plot ends affirmatively with Graff's recovering in Auntie Tratt's bathtub and ultimately deciding to reestablish purpose in his life, so does the autobiography end with quiet, ordered images that transcend the violence and chaos:

> One of Trummer's rooms is all books; one room stores the Grand Prix racer, 1939; one room has a bed, and a kitchen table. . . . The kitchen table is for sitting at, leaning on and talking over—a habit he says he can't break, even though he's alone now. . . . Believe me, Ernst Watzek-Trummer can tell you a thing or two. (252)

The books become guides to the past, present, and future, and ultimately to refinement and culture; the 1939 Grand Prix is a reminder and relic of a grand, prewar time; and Trummer still preserves and remembers history and thus can certainly "tell you a thing or two" about surviving in the modern world.

Bears sold over six thousand copies and generally received favorable reviews. The *Time* magazine critic, for instance, praised *Bears* for the "poetic grace" of its descriptions and for Irving's ability to establish a sense of place and to "make European historical anecdote live in fiction."[7] Anne Tyler admired *Bears* for its "youthful exuberance. . . . It's a gargantuan book, both in length and scope. . . . [Irving] writes with confidence and style."[8] Richard West retrospectively emphasized that *Bears* introduces readers to Irving's "now familiar signposts—bears, Vienna, the outrageously funny colliding with the shatteringly tragic."[9] At the same time, some critics praised *Bears* but noted its first-novel weaknesses. Henry S. Resnick, for instance, wrote that *Bears* is an "astonishing debut," that the novel's greatest strength is "The Notebook" section, and that Irving has "uncommon imaginative power"; however, Resnick also noted that the "first hundred pages . . . nearly spoil the entire book" because Hannes Graff's "descriptions of the people he meets . . . and his accounts of what are supposed to be hilarious going-ons are often irritatingly stilted."[10] While writing that *Bears* "must finally be judged a critical failure on major points"—its poorly developed characters, weak structure, and uncertain theme—Carol C. Harter and James R. Thompson believed that the novel's power resided in its "richly drawn scenes, moments of history intensely evoked, passages of prose already marked by a highly personal and remarkably effective style."[11]

Setting Free the Bears may have its flaws and may not be as popular as Irving's later novels. It is, however, a beginning and thus becomes a basis for understanding

Irving's later works and for appreciating his maturing world vision and literary techniques.

NOTES

1. Larry McCaffery, "An Interview with John Irving," 5–6.
2. Scott Haller, "John Irving's Bizarre World," 82.
3. John Irving, *Setting Free the Bears*, 117; hereafter cited in the text.
4. Kurt von Schuschnigg, *Austrian Requiem* (New York: Putnam, 1946), 5.
5. Gabriel Miller, *John Irving*, 33.
6. McCaffery, "Interview," 8.
7. "Wednesday's Children," *Time*, 93 (14 February 1969): 100.
8. Anne Tyler, "*Three by Irving*," *The New Republic* 182 (26 April 1980): 32.
9. Richard West, "John Irving's World After *Garp*," 30.
10. Henry S. Resnick, "At Loose Ends in the Vienna Woods," *Saturday Review*, 52 (8 February 1969): 26.
11. Carol C. Harter and James R. Thompson, *John Irving*, 20.

CHAPTER THREE

"A Happy Ending . . . Absolutely Comic": *The Water-Method Man* (1972)

Regarding *The Water-Method Man*, Irving said: "I wanted to write a book . . . with a happy ending, because I didn't feel I had a happy ending in me, and I wanted to get one. I wanted to write a book that was absolutely comic: I wanted it to be intricate and funny and clever."[1] While avoiding the violent extremes and sudden deaths that characterize his other novels, *Water-Method* is indeed Irving's truly comic novel in its settings, characterizations, themes, and techniques.

Unlike *Bears*, *Water-Method* takes place primarily in the United States but has secondary settings in Austria, namely Kaprun (a setting in *Bears*) and especially Vienna. The dual settings in the United States and Vienna foreshadow similar settings in *The 158-Pound Marriage*, *Garp*, and *The Hotel New Hampshire*. In *Bears*, violence and death stalk the Marters in Kaprun—for instance, Grandfather Marter's brother is set afire and Grandfather rides the mail sled down a ski trail to his death. In *Water-Method*, however, Kaprun augments the novel's comic vision for here protagonist Fred "Bogus" Trumper (AKA "Boggle") and Sue "Biggie" Kunft, an American Olympic giant slalom racer, fall in love. Moreover, in a delightfully slapstick scene, Trumper, whom Merrill Overturf is teaching to ski, speeds down a ski slope, launches himself into a parking lot, hurtles toward a German family of five, and lands softly in a "fleshy collision with Mother Heft, wedged between my chest and the taillights of the Mercedes."[2] As Nancy Walker notes, in Irving's other novels, such incidents "would have some shocking, tragic outcome" but are "here handled as they are in comic strips: everyone walks away unscathed."[3]

Although not directly depicting the violences spawned during and after World War II in Vienna, the plot refers indirectly to the Schonbrunn Zoo's destruction and to a German Panzer tank that resistance fighters sent to the bottom of the Danube River on New Year's Eve in 1939. Moreover, the novel's only bizarre death occurs when, in a ploy to impress and seduce Polly Crenner, an American tourist, Overturf drowns while trying to locate the tank. As will Irving's later characters, Trumper travels to Vienna, but instead of experiencing either a dead city as will Garp or one filled with neo-Nazi terrorists as do the Berry children, Trumper's Viennese sojourn is fraught with comic scenes.

The comic tone is evident first in his outlandish clothes: an ankle-length greatcoat *sans* epaulets but with a "neat, small bullet hole in the back . . . a baggy broad-shouldered suit, several yellow-white shirts . . . a six-foot purple scarf . . . a suitcase with more straps and buckles and thongs than it had room. . . . He looked like a travelling spy who had been a passenger on the Orient Express between Istanbul and Vienna since 1950" (210). Various incidents also highlight the comedy: when the *Kaffeehaus* patrons believe Trumper's suitcase contains a bomb; when Trumper, whose watch may be incorrect, asks a prostitute if she has the time; and when Trumper becomes inadvertently involved in a hashish smuggling plot.

As Vienna is for Irving's later characters, the city becomes part of Trumper's maturing process since his life at this juncture has been desultory. Although a husband, a father, and a Ph.D. candidate at the University of Iowa, Trumper cannot responsibly commit himself to anything. Bills pile up; he fabricates passages of *Akhelt and Gunnel*, his dissertation; and finally abandons home and family for Vienna to search for Merrill Overturf, whose lifestyle is even more disjointed than Trumper's. Learning that Overturf drowned while searching for the tank, Trumper then realizes that he must put meaning and purpose in his life, so he undergoes surgery for his urinary problem, responsibly completes his dissertation, and reestablishes his relationship with Tulpen, the woman whom he lives with and loves once Biggie divorces him. As Carol Harter and James Thompson note, in Vienna Trumper metaphorically kills Overturf, that "part of Trumper that denies life and therefore cannot grow . . . so that Trumper can finally transcend his own adolescent escapist tendencies."[4]

Whereas in the other novels the United States contains random mayhem and death, in *Water-Method* this setting complements the comedy. Indeed, the only death involves a duck that crashes into the Iowa City Zoo's pond—"They just get old and die, is all" (148) Colm says to soothe his father. The novel's most comical scenes occur when Trumper sells souvenirs during the Notre Dame-Iowa football game; rescues the gay who had been savagely beaten in the men's room in Benny's, a local bar; and travels with his chauffeur, Dante Calicchio, another deftly drawn comic character. Although each of these scenes attests to Irving's adeptness with extended comedy, Trumper's tryst with Lydia Kendle at the Coraville Reservoir epitomizes Irving's extended comedy technique.

When Trumper cannot make love to her because his conscience plagues him, Lydia tosses his clothes at him and roars away in her "sea-green and arklike Edsel" (160) as he stands shivering and wearing only a condom. In attempting to catch her, he runs through corn fields, cuts his feet badly on corn stalk stubble and barbed wire, and is rescued and driven back to Iowa City by two duck hunters, Harry and Eddy, also superb comic characterizations. The comedy continues when, carrying a dead duck the hunters give him, Trumper arrives home, tries to sneak into the cellar, steps on the mousetrap reserved for Risky Mouse, and lies to Biggie about being duck hunting. Trumper is unmasked when he opens his fly to urinate in front of Biggie and he has forgotten that he still wears the condom. Biggie is outraged, the condom fills, Trumper frantically searches for the scissors, Colm pushes the duck up and down the hall, and the mailman arrives with a Special Delivery letter from Trumper's father. In the later novels like *Garp*, Garp seduces the baby-sitter, Helen has as an affair with Michael Milton, and both Garp and Helen suffer for their infidelities in the car crash that blinds Duncan in one eye and kills Walt. In *Water-Method*, however, Trumper does not seduce the younger Lydia Kendle and, except for Trumper's bleeding feet, everyone remains unscathed in true comic fashion.

In *Water-Method*, the characters are more developed than those in *Bears*, and this depth is particularly evident in Trumper's characterization. Unlike Irving's other protagonists whose lives are threatened by random mayhem and death, Trumper is a comic character who is not so much concerned with surviving in a hostile world as he is with finding meaning and purpose in his life, a life symbolized by his urinary tract described as a "narrow winding road" (9). Irving pinpoints Trumper's main flaw when he describes Trumper as an "arch procrastinator like a hundred people I've known."[5] Trumper procrastinates about paying his bills, making love to Lydia Kendle, having surgery for his twisted urinary tract, completing his dissertation, committing himself to his marriage and then to his relationship with Tulpen, and even becoming a responsible adult. His two nicknames complement his procrastination. "Bogus" suggests his false sense of responsibility and life. Besides faking much of his dissertation, he also admits, "I'm a pretty good liar. . . . People who've really known me tend to believe me less and less. They tend to think I lie all the time" (8). Literally meaning to hesitate, evade, or bungle, "Boggle" suggests why he procrastinates so much, or as he tells Lydia Kendle, "No one should ever leave things up to me" (167). In attempting to evade responsibility he bungles in and out of comic situations like the Lydia Kendle fiasco and the hashish smuggling debacle.

In the comic sense, Trumper is a likeable dolt who means well but always causes problems, particularly for himself; indeed, the title of Ralph Packer's movie *Fucking Up*, an avant-garde film starring Trumper, aptly summarizes Trumper's life. Trumper's main problem, however, is that he is neither sure of who he is nor what to do with his life, or as Tulpen says:

> "No one knows you, Trumper! You don't convey anything. You don't do much, either. Things just sort

> of happen to you, and they don't add up to anything. You don't make anything of what happens to you. Ralph . . . thinks you must have a mysterious core under the surface."
>
> "And what do *you* think, Tulpen? . . . What do you think's under the surface?"
>
> "Another surface. . . . Or maybe just another surface . . . with nothing under it." (81)

Trumper is always in-between and never sure what he has done or should do next, an idea emphasized once he finishes his dissertation but too late to apply for a teaching post for that year. He wants to go to Maine to see Colm, where he would be welcomed "but couldn't live there," and he also wants to go to New York to see Tulpen "but didn't know how to introduce himself" (341). As he imagines his homecomings, his in-between stasis becomes apparent: "He had an image of how he'd like to return—as someone triumphant, like a cured cancer patient. But he couldn't decide what disease he'd had when he left so he hardly knew if he was cured" (341). Even his decision to visit Boston emphasizes his stasis: "Boston was roughly halfway between Maine and New York. And on a map of *me*, he thought, that's about where I am" (341). Significantly, however, he is *halfway* and will eventually straighten his life out once he reestablishes his relationship with Tulpen.

Another comic character is Merrill Overturf, a reckless free-spirit whose romanticism is as dated as his automobile, a Zorn-Witwer, '54. Because he is diabetic and often irresponsible about his blood-sugar levels, he also bungles in and out of comic situations—for example, lighting a cigarette's filtered end and then snuffing it out on the back of his hand because it smells bad; fashioning a "boob-loop" out of a ski pole's wrist throng and snaring women's breasts; wetting his bed on a cold night and freezing himself at the hip to the sheet. At the same time, like Trumper, Overturf shuns any responsible commitments as evidenced by his remarks to Trumper and Biggie: "You're not any fun to be with. . . . You're both in love. I don't want anything to do with either of you" (126). In that he constantly assumes various roles, Overturf mirrors Trumper's stasis, or as Trumper finally realizes:

> I'll hand it to you, Merrill; you could cultivate a marvelous look. It was the fighter-pilot look; the Grand Prix racer who'd lost his nerve, and perhaps his wife too; the former novelist with a writer's block; the ex-painter out of oil. I never knew what it was you *really* were. The unemployed actor? But you had a great look; you had the aura of an ex-hero, a former *somebody.* (308)

Trumper's comment about never knowing what Overturf was echoes Tulpen's comment about no one knowing Trumper. When Overturf drowns while searching for the tank, Trumper realizes that Overturf had been the "great illusion" (114) of his life, and Trumper can now move toward discovering purpose and meaning in life.

Cuthbert "Cuth" Bennett, Trumper's boyhood pal, is a foil for Trumper. Whereas Trumper is an irresponsible procrastinator, Cuth is a photographer of some power—"the control of it amazes me," says Trumper—is at peace with himself, and is a general handyman and caretaker on the Pillsbury Estate in Georgetown, Maine. Metaphorically, Cuth is also a caretaker. When asked, he gladly sends money so Trumper can *take care* of his mounting bills, and when Trumper abandons Biggie and Colm, Cuth takes them in and cares for them, and Trumper finally admits, "If I can't live with them, Cuth, then I'm very glad it's you. You'll take better care of them than I have" (289). In a letter, Trumper ironically underscores the difference between his and Cuth's life: "I really think you've got the life, Cuth. Better the caretaker than them who need to be cared for" (16). Until he straightens out his life, Trumper will always be one who needs to be cared for as Biggie and Tulpen do.

While no strong feminine characters appeared in *Bears*, Biggie and Tulpen in *Water-Method* foreshadow Irving's succeeding women characters. Besides denoting her physical attributes, her breasts in particular, Biggie's nickname also suggests her strong feminine virtues. She dutifully returns to her former hospital job of "bedpanning the elderly between 6 a.m. and noon" (15) to help finance Trumper's graduate program. She cleans the house, suffers the indignity at the A & P grocery when the manager refuses to accept her check, and generally tolerates Trumper's irresponsible immaturity. She is not intimidated by Trumper's father, crotchety Dr. Edmund Trumper, and besieges him with letters demanding some financial support until Trumper finishes his degree. Similarly, Tulpen is stronger and more mature than Trumper, or as he admits, "Tulpen and I are twenty-eight, but she's really older than I am; she has outgrown having to talk about herself" (10). She pays the bills, buys the groceries, comforts him as did Biggie when he is melancholy, and also tolerates his procrastinations. Regardless of whether or not Trumper will assume both fatherly and financial obligations, Tulpen decides to have his child, whom she names Merrill because Trumper seemed so fond of the name. In their strength, determination, and feminine virtues, Biggie and Tulpen become prototypes for, to name a few, Utch [*The 158-Pound Marriage*], Jenny Fields [*Garp*], Franny Berry [*Hotel New Hampshire*], and Candy [*Cider House*]. Finally, Biggie and Tulpen are significant for the novel's family theme.

While in *Bears*, the Hilke family forms a temporary bulwark against life's forces, the family as a stabilizing center is a major theme in *Water-Method*. At the Pillsbury Estate assemble three families: Trumper, Tulpen, and baby Merrill; Biggie, Cuth, Colm, and baby Anna; Ralph Packer and Matje, his pregnant wife. When the weather turns cold, foul, and foggy, the families form one big family and cook, eat, drink, play together, and individually help Colm adjust to so much company. Amid the contentment, family togetherness, and good company, Trumper begins to write about his life, to put it into perspective. Significantly, too, he realizes that he is "actually at peace with himself for the first time in his life" (361). From his inner peace, he resolves his differences with Biggie and each feels comfortable with the other, and he finally tells Tulpen that he loves her.

As adjunct to the family theme, Trumper typifies the overprotective parents in Irving's fiction. He even stops riding motorcycles once Colm is born because, as he says, children give him a "sudden sense . . . of mortality" (144). Although he may be at loose ends and generally irresponsible, he tries to protect Colm. When Colm rides his tricycle around the block, for example, Trumper hides behind bushes and follows. When Biggie sends Colm for a visit, Trumper imagines numerous tragedies befalling the airplane, and in New York Trumper prefers cabs so that Colm would not "see any subway happenings'' (187). Trumper even checks on Colm during the night: ''What I mind about children is that they're so vulnerable, so fragile-looking. Colm: I get up in the night to make sure your breathing hasn't stopped'' (48). Trumper's selfless concern for Colm becomes the force that brings Trumper back to Tulpen and baby Merrill.

Except for *Bears* and *Garp*, *Water-Method* is perhaps Irving's most intricately plotted novel: ''Technically, in terms of stuntsmanship and fiction, I think *The Water-Method Man* is a much more energetic piece of work. In terms of all those manipulations of point of view and tense. I don't claim it as an experimental novel, but it's the closest I will ever come to doing that kind of thing.''[6] The plot alternates between the first- and third-person point of view. The third-person perspective details Trumper's past: his youth when he and Cuth catch the clap from Elsbeth Malkas; his sojourn in Austria when he falls in love with Biggie; and his experiences at the University of Iowa as his marriage collapses in 1969 and he flees to Vienna to find Overturf. The first-person narrative occurs in the present as he lives with Tulpen, returns to finish his Ph.D., has the surgery, and gathers for the Throgsgafen Day festivities. In addition, some plot elements are developed in Ralph Packer's *Fucking Up* which parodies Trumper's life. Even Trumper's travels from Iowa to Vienna, to New York, to Iowa, and then to Maine reflect his desultory life.

If refrains ''mark how far you've come'' and ''forewarn you about where you're going,''[7] the only verbal refrain in *Water-Method* refers to Trumper's urinary tract as a ''narrow, winding road,'' which is also the novel's major symbol. Besides indicating his life and one of his problems, this refrain indicates why his procrastination hampers straightening out his life. In the opening section, he admits "I want to change" (10), but he procrastinates and refuses to take Tulpen's advice: "Surgery. . . . If something *can* be fixed, fix it" (8). Instead of surgery, Trumper opts for the water-method treatment, which requires him to drink large quantities of water before and after sex to flush out his urinary tract. Moreover, after the surgery, Trumper continues to straighten out his life by translating *Akhelt and Gunnel*, the novel's action refrain. Throughout the plot's past and present scenes, Trumper is always trying to complete his dissertation. Although in the past he irresponsibly fabricates the translation, he eventually completes a scholarly translation and thus takes the next step in amending his life, reestablishing his relationship with Tulpen and baby Merrill.

Whereas *Bears* and *Garp* contain several narratives within the main narrative, Trumper's translation of *Akhelt and Gunnel* provides the only narrative within the main plot. In true epic fashion, the poem is about warfare, death, revenges, Sprog (a monstrous Devil's Toad), and the dissolution of Thak's kingdom. These dire events contrast with Trumper's comedic world. For instance, Sprog is "deballed with a battle ax" for attempting to make love to Gunnel, but nothing that terrible results when Trumper tries to make love to Lydia Kendle. While the epic ends in bloody dissolution as Gunnel goes insane and decapitates various people including Akhelt, the Throgsgafen celebration emphasizes love and family solidarity. In other incidents, *Akhelt and Gunnel* complements the novel's plot. When Akhelt wishes to take six-year-old Alexrulf on a warring expedition, Gunnel refuses because during the campaign Akhelt will surely "take a woman. . . . Just to fuck . . . she won't be a mother to him" (181). When

Biggie sends Colm to visit, she insists that Trumper not make love to Tulpen so that Colm would not be confused about a mother's true role. In later novels, the narratives within the main plot will be more numerous and more sophisticated as they illuminate various plot incidents.

Water-Method contains some Irvingesque motifs that receive fuller treatment in later novels. In Vienna, for instance, Trumper thinks about the Viennese prostitutes who, as they grow older and less attractive, move out through the city's districts until they are "mauled by factory workers and technical high school students for half the fare they had once charged" (218), a theme more poignantly rendered in Charlotte's characterization in *Garp*. While not a major metaphor as in the next two novels, wrestling emphasizes Trumper's life: "His potential was considered 'vast,' but he must learn to conquer his regrettable concentration span. . . . His wrestling performance? Undistinguished" (57).

In true comic fashion, *Water-Method* ends affirmatively with a typical Irvingesque epilogue, "The Old Friends Assemble for Throgsgafen Day," an old Low Norse holiday somewhat similar to America's Thanksgiving. As symbolized by the abundant food, drink, good-natured banter, and especially by the two babies and Matje's pregnancy, this epilogue celebrates life's bounteous blessings and Trumper's reassimilation into life's flow. The affirmative tone is particularly evident when the three families gather for breakfast and Trumper reflects: "So what if dog puke still lurked unseen in the laundry room! In good company we can be brave. Mindful of his scars, his old harpoons and things, Bogus Trumper smiled cautiously at all the good flesh around him" (365). Trumper has finally learned from his experiences (his old scars) and is at peace with himself and the world even if it is a cautious peace. While not as foreboding as the forces in the other novels, the lurking, unseen dog puke represents life's forces, but as long as people have friends and family—the good "company" and "flesh"—life is indeed meaningful and purposeful.

Water-Method sold 6,906 copies and was selected for the *New York Times* list as one of the best novels for 1972.[8] Yet critics differed regarding the novel's strength and weaknesses. While Anne Tyler claimed that *Water-Method* is a "pure joy" and praised its "irrepressible comedy,"[9] Paul Majkut wrote that *Water-Method* was "not exceptionally funny, though it is typical of what has come to pass as funny these days in the American comic novel. That is, it is light, well-trained, even risque, and it avoids every real human issue present throughout the land, throughout the world. . . . [The author and his book] are the product of 'creative writing': both are stylistically and thematically, if the terms can be applied here, rooted in the Writer's Workshop at the University of Iowa; both are natural corn."[10] The *New Yorker* reviewer criticized *Water-Method* because it flipped "back and forth through [Trumper's] life as if it were telling three or four stories at once," and although it was "often three or four times as funny as most novels," the book lost "its grip on reality" as Trumper became a "lovable soup-head telling us that life is just great."[11] On the other hand, Jan Carew noted that in *Water-Method* Irving reasserted "his inventiveness, wit and obvious ability to devour new experiences . . . and convert them into imaginative symbols and literary episodes" that assumed a "cohesive and even more meaningful form" once the reader puts the novel down and allows "some time to elapse."[12] Carol Harter and James Thompson believed that *Water-Method* indicated Irving's maturing literary talents in "every respect—especially in the creation of strong characters and in the control of tone. . . . And while the novel lacks the massive quality of *Garp* or the dream dimension of *Hotel New Hampshire* or the serious 'polemic' of *Cider House*, it remains Irving's most complex novel in terms of narrative technique."[13]

If *Bears* is a Baedeker to Irving's fiction, then *The Water-Method Man* marks Irving's progress as a writer and thus provides a basis for evaluating his succeeding works. His next novel, *The 158-Pound Marriage* continues to develop Irving's literary techniques and world vision.

NOTES

1. Greil Marcus, "John Irving: The World of *The World According to Garp*," 72.
2. John Irving, *The Water-Method Man*, 99; hereafter cited in the text.
3. Nancy Walker, "John Irving," 1419.
4. Carol C. Harter and James R. Thompson, *John Irving*, 49.
5. Larry McCaffery, "An Interview with John Irving," 8.
6. Michael Priestley, "An Interview with John Irving," 503.
7. Laura de Coppet, "An Interview with John Irving," 44.
8. Richard West, "John Irving's World After *Garp*," 30.
9. Anne Tyler, "*Three by Irving*," *The New Republic* 182 (26 April 1980): 33, 32.
10. Paul Majkut, *Best Sellers*, 32 (July 1972): 156.
11. "Books Briefly Noted," *The New Yorker*, 48 (22 July 1972): 78.
12. Jan Carew, *New York Times Book Review*, 10 September 1972, 46.
13. Harter and Thompson, *John Irving*, 40.

CHAPTER FOUR

"I Lost My Sense of Humor": *The 158-Pound Marriage* (1974)

Irving said he was reading Ford Madox Ford's *The Good Soldier* and John Hawkes's *The Blood Oranges* as he worked on *The 158-Pound Marriage*: "If I'd not read those two books, I would not have written *The 158-Pound Marriage*. That's the kind of period I was in at the time: everything I read was a *labor* and it made me *angry*. It was like I lost my sense of humor."[1] If *The Water-Method Man* is Irving's most comic novel, then *The 158-Pound Marriage* is Irving's darkest work, especially in its characterizations, incidents, and themes.

The 158-Pound Marriage has dual settings, in the United States and in Austria. As in *Bears*, the Austrian settings in *Marriage* depict the aftermath of the *Anschluss* and World War II, but the fury and violence occur primarily in Eichbuchl, where Utch, the narrator's wife, is born. For example, after Utch's father is killed for sabotaging Messerschmitts on the Wiena Neustadt runway, the *SS Standarte* arrive in the village, rape Utch's mother, and before leaving order the villagers to watch her closely. Later, some village men rape Utch's mother again but are not formally charged because they claimed they were following orders of the SS. When a bombing raid destroys her orchard, Frau Haslinger goes temporarily insane, hacks at herself with a pruning hook, and has to be restrained in a huge apple bin where some village men rape her. However, this rape is "considered a fantasy due to her derangement at the loss of the apple crop."[2] The cycle of violence continues when the Russians arrive in 1945: they lay waste Eichbuchl, rape women, butcher men, commit other atrocities, and one of them kills Utch's mother. The unconscionable terror and violence in Eichbuchl suggest the even wider destructive swaths occurring everywhere before, during, and after World War II.

Instead of detailing the violence in Vienna as he did in *Bears* during and after the *Anschluss*, Irving alludes to various incidents in *Marriage*: the seventy-six thousand arrested in the Gestapo's first dragnet, the "generation gap" created by the war, the rapes and machine-gunnings during the Russian occupation, and the nefarious Benno Blum Gang, which liquidates anti-Soviet dissidents. Vienna's image becomes less sinister, therefore, because it is rebuilding and progressing toward the future. Even the Benno Blum Gang's actions become lightened when Utch's personal bodyguard, a Blum gangster, selflessly protects her for twenty-five years because he has fallen in love with her. Utch flourishes and matures into a beautiful, cultured woman who falls in love with the narrator when they meet in Vienna; Severin Winter and Edith Fuller also meet and fall in love in Vienna. As it will become for Garp's family after Walt's death, Vienna in *Marriage* becomes a refuge when, in the novel's conclusion, Utch and her children, the Winters and their children, and even the narrator return to Vienna to heal their *Weltschmerz* (World Hurt), or as the narrator emphasizes,

"Vienna has a fabulous history of treaties; the truces made here over the years run long and deep" (244).

In addition, Irving technically establishes subtle links between Vienna's violent history in *Bears* and the incidents in *Marriage*. Both novels, for instance, refer to the first wave of Gestapo arrests; the parcelling of Vienna among the Americans, British, and Russians; the rapes and machine-gunnings during the Russian occupation; Joseph Stalin's death; and the end of the ten-year Russian occupation. Another link is that actress Katrina Marek, who is seven months pregnant with Severin, flees Vienna the day before the *Anschluss*, Black Friday, March 11, 1938, thus forcing the cancellation of *Antigone* in which she starred; in *Bears* Zahn Glanz parks his taxi under the poster advertising Marek's role in *Antigone*. Kurt Winter, Severin's father, may have driven editor Lennhoff to Hungary and may have even freed the Schonbrunn Zoo animals in 1945—feats attributed to Glanz in *Bears*. In both novels, the Benno Blum Gang stalks Vienna—"they transported people—forever" (49). Chancellor Figl claims that the government can only write "disappeared" by the names of missing persons. Dressed in the Austrian Eagle costume, Glanz frightens laundress Drexa Neff in *Bears*, and laundress Neff takes care of Utch in *Marriage*. Both Utch and Severin live in a Schwindgasse apartment, the same neighborhood in which the Marters lived in *Bears*. While these links reemphasize the cataclysmic events that shaped Vienna's history, they also indicate that Irving is extending his analysis of the violence that he sees at the heart of the modern world and that he will deal with in his next two novels.

In *Marriage*, the United States setting occurs on a New England college campus and thus foreshadows the New

Hampshire and Maine settings in his later novels. Although the plot alludes to President John F. Kennedy's assassination, mayhem and death do not stalk the characters' lives, and the only violence occurs when the Winters' daughters are cut badly but not fatally as the shower door shatters while they play in the bathtub. Irving does, however, focus on a metaphorical violence as he analyzes the mate-swapping fads of the 1960s and 1970s. Both couples in *Marriage* think a *menage a quatre* will rejuvenate their eight-year-old marriages, and while it temporarily provides sexual pleasure and satisfies lust, the quaternion almost destroys both marriages and emotionally scars its participants, or as Utch finally admits, "It just gets uglier" (219).

Except for several well-drawn minor characters—Katrina Marek, Audrey Cannon, Willy and Heinrich, and Zivan Knezevich and Vaso Trianovich—*Marriage* spotlights the two couples, and the most unappealing of the four characters is the unnamed narrator. Irving says, "I felt in *The 158-Pound Marriage* as if I were writing about people I didn't like, especially the narrator."[3] The narrator lacks the humor and compassion that will characterize Irving's later protagonists, such as Garp, John Berry, and Johnny Wheelwright. The narrator is, in fact, a self-centered, sarcastic bore who learns almost nothing from history—he has a Ph.D. in history and writes historical novels—nor does he learn much from the *ménage à quatre*. Often he is so immersed in his sarcastic views and self-importance that he neglects his children, and he has had extra-marital affairs with Sally Frotsch, "an independent study" student, and Mrs. Stewart, a divorcee. In addition, the narrator always makes faulty judgments as evidenced when he forcibly takes Utch to the gym because he thinks

Severin may be having another affair to gain "leverage" again on Edith. He also mistakenly thinks Edith loves and will miss him once the swapping terminates. Although he accuses Severin of having tunnel vision as a result of the wrestling rituals, the narrator suffers from a more damning tunnel vision, or as Utch finally tells him, "You know *you*. . . . That's all you know" (231). In the novel's conclusion, however, the narrator realizes what may be a saving grace when he admits that his children are important after all, when he has nightmares about Jack and Bart, and when he goes to Vienna because "It's a way to be near the children" (244).

Born in 1938, Utchka, the narrator's wife, becomes a child of the *Anschluss* and its aftermath. After her father is shot as a saboteur, her mother hides Utch inside a cow's carcass to protect her from the pillaging and raping Russians. When one Russian threatens to burn the barn in which Utch is hidden, her mother kills the Russian with a trenching spade and is in turn shot by another Russian. Although originally named Anna Agati Thalhammer, her name changes to Utchka, which means *calf* in Russian, when she slides out of the carcass as it is being lifted onto a truck. Orphaned by the war, she becomes the ward of Captain Kudashvili who takes her to live in the Russian section of Vienna. Although she is orphaned again when Kudashvili dies in the Hungarian uprising, Utch blossoms and matures, and as a guide in the *Kunsthistorisches* Museum, she falls in love with the narrator. Because of her European experiences, she is naturally drawn to Severin Winter once the mate swapping begins, falls in love with him, and so is the most emotionally scarred person of the quaternion. Gabriel Miller argues that Utch is not a "convincing character . . . Things seem to happen to her—she mostly gets drunk and falls asleep—though she does rouse herself to fall in love with Severin Winter.''[4] However, she also rouses herself at the end of the novel, decides to live apart from her husband, and takes her sons to Vienna to assuage her scarred emotions. Her decision is, nevertheless, a positive step toward reestablishing purpose and meaning in her family's life.

Like Utch, Severin Winter is a child of the *Anschluss* and its aftermath. To protect her unborn fetus, Katrina Marek flees to London where Severin is born, and they both return to Vienna after the war. When Katrina dies, Severin is raised by foster fathers, Zivan Knezevich and Vaso Trianovich, former Chetnik freedom fighters and 1936 Olympic wrestlers, who persuade Severin to attend the University of Iowa. There he becomes a runner-up in the middleweight division of the Big Ten wrestling championships. He returns to Vienna and eventually meets Edith when he becomes her unofficial guide and takes her to various art museums. He wants to return to the United States because, as he says, ''Everything and everyone is dying here'' (40), so he and Edith marry, and he becomes the university wrestling coach and a German professor. Like Utch, Severin is always conscious of the children and takes better care of them than does Edith, a fact the narrator underscores when he sarcastically says that Severin's ''ambition was to be a *wife*'' (110). Severin also knows the danger inherent in mate swapping and even remarks, ''I guess I feel that I have to do the worrying for all of us . . . because no one else seems worried about anything'' (64). Furthermore, he only agrees to the mate swapping to assuage his guilt and ease Edith's pain, which resulted from his affair with Audrey Cannon. When he realizes that the mate swapping is getting out of control—

wrestlers like to be in control—he begins to undermine the relationships. He eventually succeeds when he takes Utch to the wrestling room, and when Edith finds out, she is devastated, "How could he *do* that!" she cried. "He must have known how he'd hurt me" (176).

Edith shares common interests and backgrounds with the narrator. She comes from an affluent family—the "New York Fullers"—attends a Paris prep school, and then Sarah Lawrence College. She is also a writer and even completes a novel during the turmoil of the mate swapping. Like the narrator, she is not very concerned with her two daughters, Dorabella and Fiordiligi, usually never hears what they say to her, and often confuses their names when she does talk to them. Edith is a more dynamic character than Utch and refuses to kowtow to Severin's chauvinism, although she loves him. Instead of quietly suffering when she catches Severin with Audrey Cannon, she beats, kicks, scratches, bites him and even mashes his toes with her heavy Tyrolian boots. Later, when Severin forces her to go to the Big Ten championships because he does not trust her, she tries to seduce George James Bender because, as she says about Severin, "I wanted to teach him that he couldn't cram his life down my throat and not leave me free to live mine" (217). When the narrator egotistically believes she will suffer because the swapping ended, she adamantly says, "I'm all right, I'm not suffering. I'm not in love with you" (214). When Edith finally goes to the wrestling room with Severin, they both begin their recovery process, a process that will be completed once they return to Vienna. In her love for Severin and her determination to be an individual, she is another prototype for Irving's later heroines.

Rather than dominating the plot, the family theme in *Marriage* symbolically hovers in the background and emphasizes the selfishness inherent in the wife-swapping motif. For instance, Dorabella, Fiordiligi, Jack, and Bart are either asleep at night when the mates swap, or "farmed out" as during the Cape Cod weekend, or are attending a party, or having swimming lessons. This lack of parental concern is most apparent in the narrator's and Edith's actions. When the couples are together in the Winters' kitchen and all of the children are there, Fiordiligi asks her mother a question four times before Severin screams from the stove to make Edith aware of the question. As usual, Edith confuses the names and calls Fiordiligi, Dorabella—"Right name, wrong daughter" (29). Like Edith, the narrator often forgets he has children and confesses, "I admit that my own sense of family suffered from our foursome. I remember the children least of all, and that bothers me" (119).

In contrast, for Utch and especially Severin, the children are important. In the kitchen scene, for example, the narrator emphasizes that Severin heard Fiordiligi's question, and Utch also "heard everything the children ever said" (29). After the bathtub accident, Utch must remind her husband, "Your children are more important to you than anything" (225), and he can only agree with her. The role of children in the family theme is especially evident in Severin's characterization. He constantly worries about his children and family life, "Edith knew that Severin Winter's sense of family was more ferocious than most" (119).

Severin also becomes a mother and father image, a role that Garp will assume. Severin's father-mother role is symbolized in a scene in which he sleeps among the four children:

> The groggy children were slowly waking; they curled and snuggled against him as if he were a large pillow or a friendly dog—and Severin Winter lay among them in Edith's gown, looking like a transvestite weight lifter dropped through the roof of an elementary school like a benign bomb. (124)

In interpreting this scene, Carol C. Harter and James R. Thompson note, "Severin Winter's ease in adapting to both the maternal and paternal, the masculine and feminine aspects of himself and of human experience, is a sign of his durability, his complexity, and finally his strength."[5] These virtues will eventually be the catalyst for his deciding that the mate swapping must end.

Irving emphasizes the significance of parental devotion and responsibility through several minor characters. Not only does Utch's mother hide her in a cow to protect her from the Russians, but she selflessly sacrifices her own life when she kills the Russian who threatens to burn the barn. Captain Kudashvili becomes a strong father figure for Utch, dutifully walks her to school every day, and orders members of the Benno Blum Gang to protect her. Drexa Neff underscores Kudashvili's strongest virtue when she says, he is a "moral man, even though he is a Russian, and a moral man is more than some of you can call your fathers" (48). When Kudashvili is killed, the Benno Blum gangster with the hole in his cheek becomes Utch's surrogate but secret father, and because he promised Kudashvili, the gangster protects Utch for twenty-five years until she marries the narrator. Even then he threatens to kill the narrator if he does not take good care of Utch. In contrast to Edith's lack of concern, Katrina Marek's motherly role is evident when she flees Vienna and the war to protect Severin. For that matter, Zivan Knezevich and Vaso Trianovich responsibly protect Severin just as the Benno Blum gangsters protect Utch. Such selfless devotion and responsibility underscore the unconscionable qualities inherent in the quaternion, qualities that the narrator and Utch ironically recognized before they married:

> We spoke of fidelity as the only way. We considered conventional "affairs" as double deceptions, degrading to everyone involved. We regarded "arrangements" as callous—the kind of premeditation that is opposite to genuine passion. How people could conceive of such things was beyond us. We speculated on the wisdom of couple "swapping"; it hardly seemed wise. In fact, it seemed an admission of an unforgivable boredom, utterly decadent and grossly wasteful of the erotic impulse. (160)

Although not a major metaphor in *Water-Method*, wrestling becomes a significant metaphor in *Marriage*. The novel's title refers to the 158-pound weight division for Severin and George James Bender. The wrestling metaphor also furnishes the titles of the second, third, fourth, fifth, sixth, eighth, and ninth chapters. Furthermore, the wrestling room has womblike connotations: it has two "roaring blow-heaters" and the walls and floor are covered with crimson and white pads and mats. In addition, Severin often looks in at his wrestlers "like a father observing his children in some incubator phase" (180), and the womblike connotations are also apparent when, before all home matches, Severin marches the wrestlers "through the long connecting tunnel to the new gym," where they emerge into the bright, noisy gym (69). Besides being a place where the wrestlers learn to endure pain, the wrestling room is also a place for love and is suggested by the chapter's title, "The Wrestling-Room

Lover.'' Severin makes love to Audrey Cannon and to Utch in the wrestling room. At the end of the novel, Utch says the wrestling room is a place where she can ''be alone . . . a good place to think—to just rest'' (226). In the wrestling room, too, Utch becomes orgasmic again when she and her husband make love there; moreover, Severin and Edith begin healing their emotional scars when they too make love in the wrestling room.

As implied in the titles of Chapter Four, ''Preliminary Positions,'' and Chapter Six, ''Who's on Top? Where's the Bottom?,'' the wrestling metaphor complements the mate swapping. The couples spend most of their time, for example, in metaphorical wrestling positions while making love in beds, on couches, in showers, or on wrestling mats. In one scene, Edith and Severin indulge in a lovemaking marathon that leaves Edith hurting ''all over, everywhere,'' and Severin says, ''That's how it feels after a match'' (77). Lovemaking between Utch and Severin also suggests the wrestling metaphor: Utch's clothes are strewn everywhere, the mattress is half off the bed, the ''sheets knotted like a great balled fist which I imagine pounding the mattress askew'' (126), and food and empty bottles litter the room.

A wrestling metaphor also emphasizes the petty viciousness of the mate swapping, especially between Severin and Edith, who initiate and then terminate the quaternion. As long as the sexual encounters remain equal, then neither one gains ''leverage,'' which the narrator calls, ''Another wrestling term. I didn't like its application to couples'' (140). Severin's affair with Audrey Cannon gives him leverage first, but when Edith learns of the affair, she warns Severin: ''But now I've got the leverage on you. I can feel it, and you can too. And I don't like having it any better than you do, so I'm going to use it and then it will be gone'' (195). When Severin takes Utch to the wrestling room and when Edith attempts to seduce Bender, each is vying for leverage. When Severin and Edith realize that their actions may destroy their genuine love for each other, the leverage ceases, the swapping terminates, and the match is over.

The only refrain in *Marriage* is ''the whole thing,'' which refers to the quaternion. As the couples discuss the possibilities of mate swapping, they decide that each one must agree to ''the whole thing.'' They decide that as long as no one gets hurt and as long as ''Nobody's going to leave anybody, or run off with somebody else'' (64), the *ménage à quatre* would be ''exciting, it was the newness of meeting someone—that old romance was eight years old, more or less, for all of us—that was so enhancing'' (63). The sexual satisfaction climaxes on the Cape Cod weekend in sexual abandon in what the narrator believes is a ''beginning'' but which Severin says is ''just a holiday . . . like calling time out'' from ''children and reality'' (99, 106). The refrain appears later when Severin decides to end the arrangement and tells the narrator: Utch ''knows I didn't really want the whole thing, and she knows you were thinking more about yourself than about her. We were all thinking more about ourselves than about Utch. And you were all thinking more about yourselves than about me'' (236). The entire mate-swapping agreement is based, not on love, but lust, an idea Utch emphasizes when she admits, ''I don't even know if we were lovers . . . I think we were just fuckers'' (205). Even though the ''whole thing'' is terminated, the damning implications still persist, or to quote Utch, ''It just goes on and on'' (219). And so Edith avenges herself against Severin; Severin bruises Edith's face with a book;

Utch cannot become orgasmic, and she abandons her husband. The narrator, who is angry with Severin for ending the swapping, ironically hopes that Bender will throw "the whole thing" during the wrestling championships (213).

Although not as ebullient as in *Water-Method* and the later novels, *Marriage* ends affirmatively. In the concluding chapter, both couples at least begin their healing processes when they make love in the wrestling room. Just as Utch becomes orgasmic in the last place she had an orgasm, symbolically both couples return to Vienna where they first fell in love. The narrator may not have learned much from his experiences, but he finally realizes that he misses Utch and the children, and the family often becomes a saving grace for Irving's characters. Whether he and Utch will reconcile is a moot point, but significantly Utch has written to him and has even returned his passport, so a potential reconciliation exists in Vienna with its history of truces that "run long and deep" (244). Finally, the concluding sentence suggests that the narrator may have a second chance with his marriage and family: "If cuckolds catch a second wind, I am eagerly waiting for mine" (245).

The 158-Pound Marriage sold only 2,560 copies, and Irving blamed the failure of *Marriage* as well as the "commercial failure" of his first two novels on Random House's "reluctance to properly promote his books."[6] At any rate, critics were not as kind to *Marriage* as they were to *Bears* and *Water-Method*. Criticism of *Marriage* ranged from Pearl K. Bell, who faulted its poorly developed characters and theme,[7] to Nancy Walker, who thought the plot suffered because Irving did not combine tragedy and comedy, which resulted in a "flatness rather than peaks and valleys of emotion which Irving is capable of evoking.''[8] Although Carol C. Harter and James K. Thompson believed that *Marriage* suffered because Irving ''self-consciously'' patterned it on Ford Madox Ford's *The Good Soldier* and John Hawkes's *The Blood Oranges*,[9] Charles Nicol said *Marriage* was ''all muscle, all confidence'' and did not ''suffer in comparison'' with *The Good Soldier* and *The Blood Oranges*.[10]

In *Marriage*, Irving does not juxtapose the comic with the tragic, and except for Edith's short story that does not illuminate the main plot, Irving does not include any narratives-within-the-narrative. The novel's main strength, however, lies in Irving's relentless analysis of the damning effects inherent in mate swapping, and such relentless probing makes *Marriage* Irving's darkest novel in its characterizations, incidents, and themes. Significantly, however, *The 158-Pound Marriage* becomes a necessary bridge between the pure comedy of *Water-Method* and *Garp* and its nicely balanced comedy and horror.

NOTES

1. Greil Marcus, ''John Irving,'' 72; Gabriel Miller's *John Irving* provides interesting comparisons between *The Good Soldier*, *The Blood Oranges*, and *The 158-Pound Marriage*.
2. John Irving, *The 158-Pound Marriage*, 5; hereafter cited in the text.
3. Larry McCaffery, ''An Interview with John Irving,'' 8.
4. Miller, *John Irving*, 83.
5. Carol C. Harter and James R. Thompson, *John Irving*, 67.
6. Richard West, ''John Irving's World After *Garp*,'' 30.
7. Pearl K. Bell, ''Lovers and Losers,'' *New Leader*, 57 (25 November 1974): 14.
8. Nancy Walker, ''John Irving,'' 1420.
9. Harter and Thompson, *John Irving*, 56–57.
10. Charles Nicol, ''Wrestling,'' *National Review*, 27 (24 October 1975): 1187–88.

CHAPTER FIVE

"The Best of the Four": *The World According to Garp* (1976)

Irving said that *The World According to Garp* "is far and away the best of the four published books; there's no question about this in my mind. *Garp* seemed to bring together a lot of things I'd only been getting started in my other books. It summarized the other books for me, finished the cycle I had started."[1] When compared with the preceding three novels, *Garp* is stylistically and artistically superior, and while reintroducing Irvingesque settings, characters, themes, and techniques, these elements are more richly and fully integrated into the novel's plot and depth.

Garp reintroduces, for example, dual settings, New Hampshire and Vienna. However, Irving only alludes to the *Anschluss*-spawned violence that shaped Vienna's past. When Garp and Jenny arrive in Vienna, for example, Garp notices the generation gap created by the war and Russian occupation:

> There were very few people in Vienna who were even the same age as Garp. Not many Viennese were born in 1943; for that matter, not many Viennese were born

> from the start of the Nazi occupation in 1938 through the end of war in 1945. And although there were a surprising number of babies born out of rapes, not many Viennese *wanted* babies until after 1955—the end of the Russian occupation.[2]

In addition, the plot refers to the Schonbrunn Zoo's "war ruins" that give Garp the "eerie impression that the zoo still existed in Vienna's war period," and in another scene, Garp feels the "holes from machine-gun fire in the stone walls of his apartment lobby in Schwindgasse" (167). While these oblique references recall the more detailed violence in *Bears* and *Marriage*, they also become part of the novel's life-death cycles. As Garp notes, Vienna is a "museum housing a dead city . . . Vienna was in its death phase" (86). Furthermore, Irving symbolizes Vienna's death phase in Charlotte, the aging prostitute whose sexual organs are slowly being ravaged by disease—"her sex is sick," says another prostitute. According to Gabriel Miller, Charlotte represents "Vienna, clinging to the memory of a glamorous past, while hiding the scars occasioned by its less glamorous moments."[3]

Years later, when Garp returns with his family, Vienna has changed: "The Viennese appeared well fed and comfortable with luxuries that looked new to Garp; the city was years away from the Russian occupation, the memory of the war, the reminders of ruins. If Vienna had been dying, or already dead, in his time there with his mother, Garp felt something new but common had grown in the old city's place" (341–42). Vienna's rising from its own ruins complements the bildungsroman theme in that Garp learns from Vienna's past that there is life after death, that life indeed must go on, and that he must refuse to be victimized by life's forces. Or, as the narrator observes, "It was Garp's experience to live in a city that made him feel peculiar to be eighteen years old. This must have made him grow older faster" (86). That Garp will learn from the city's history is evident when he writes to Helen Holm: Vienna "lay still and let me look at it, and think about it, and look again. In a *living* city, I could have never noticed so much" (86).

Irving shifts the *Anschluss*-spawned violence, however, to the United States where the violence seems more irrational and universal, and manifests itself in rapes, self-mutilations, extremist groups, murders, and bizarre deaths. As Garp flies home to attend his martyred mother's funeral, for instance, he returns "home to be famous in his violent country" (349), where he too will be murdered. Unlike the references to potential violence in *Water-Method* and *Marriage*, the United States setting in *Garp* contains random violence and death that stalk the lives of Garp, his family, friends, and acquaintances, "In the world according to Garp, we are all terminal cases" (437), a quotation emphasizing life's brevity as well as the violence and death at the core of Irving's world vision. The horror stalking the postmodern world is apparent in the number of bizarre, often violent, deaths in the plot. Jenny Fields and Garp are assassinated; Walt dies in a car crash; Harrison and Alice Fletcher die in a plane crash during the Christmas holidays; Ernie Holm dies of a heart attack while looking at *Crotch Shots*, a pornographic magazine; Mr. Tinch freezes to death; Cushie Percy dies in childbirth; Ellen James drowns in the treacherous undertow of Dog's Head Harbor; and Duncan Garp chokes to death on an olive while laughing too hard at one of his own jokes. The violence and bizarre deaths not only recall incidents in *Bears* but also foreshadow what will typically plague Irving's characters in his next novels.

Irving said that with *Garp* he created characters he "genuinely admired and cared for; this was a major breakthrough for me."[4] The novel's central focus is T. S. Garp, who has fears and setbacks not unlike those of Siggy, Hannes, Trumper, and Severin, but who also embodies their strengths and virtues. Like Irving's other characters, Garp is a semi-orphan since his father, Technical Sergeant Garp, dies from war wounds after Garp's inception, and Garp has surrogate father figures like Dean Bodger, Mr. Tinch, and Ernie Holm. Like Siggy, Trumper, and the unnamed narrator of *Marriage*, Garp is a writer, but unlike these other protagonists, Garp's profession is writing. John Wolf, his editor and friend, praises Garp's dedication: "He started out daring to write about the *world*—when he was just a *kid*, for Christ's sake, he still took it on" (424). Even more so than Severin, Garp is a believable paternal-maternal figure, who cooks, cleans, and cares for Duncan, Walt, and Jenny. Like Trumper, Garp is an overprotective father who watches his children while they sleep, secretly checks on Duncan when he spends the night with Ralph at Mrs. Ralph's house, has nightmares about their safety, and when Walt has a serious cold Garp sleeps with his head near Walt's chest in case the boy stops breathing during the night. Although Garp seduces several baby-sitters and he, Helen, and the Fletchers indulge in mate swapping, Garp's marriage and love for Helen remain stable and life-affirming, even though he and Helen suffer for their infidelities in the car crash that breaks Garp's jaw, blinds Duncan in one eye, and kills Walt. Furthermore, these experiences are integrated into the bildungsroman motif that traces Garp's rites of passage from childhood through adolescence to adulthood.

Unlike his prototypes, who are cautiously optimistic, Garp, because he lives in a violent world, learns from his experiences and develops a positive code for living purposefully despite life's sometimes overwhelming forces.

Helen Holm is likewise a semi-orphan since her mother, also a nurse, abandons her. Because her father coaches wrestling, Helen spends a "lifetime of three-hour afternoons sitting in wrestling rooms" (56) where she reads—Helen and Jenny are Steering School's avid readers—and where she eventually meets Garp. Although not as detailed as Garp's life, Irving's relating of Helen's experiences are integral parts of the bildungsroman technique because she also moves from adolescence to adulthood. Helen initiates the mate-swapping venture in an effort to help Harrison Fletcher, an English Department colleague, outgrow an affair with one of his students. During the mate swapping, Garp and Alice love each other, and Harrison loves Helen, but, unlike Utch in *Marriage*, Helen does not fall in love. Moreover, Helen terminates this quaternion because she enjoys "it the least of them" and "suffered the most" (158). However, because she is bored with Garp and their marriage, Helen initiates an affair with Michael Milton, a smug, "unlikeable" graduate student, but she controls the relationship. When she realizes that Garp knows and is deeply hurt, she terminates the affair. Ironically, both Helen and Garp become aware at this juncture of how much they love each other: Garp "thought to himself how much he loved Helen and would *never* be unfaithful to her again—never hurt her like this. . . . At the same moment Helen felt her conscience clear. Her love for Garp was very fine" (265).

Jenny Fields typifies Irving's strong, independent female characters who live their own lives but never lose their femininity. Although from a socially prominent, affluent Boston family who wants her to marry well, Jenny becomes a nurse and is interested in neither men nor marriage. When a soldier tries to molest her in a movie, for example, she slices his arm with a scalpel. Because she wants a child without the attendant marital bothers, she makes love to the comatose Technical Sergeant Garp before he dies from his war wounds. Jenny is also a very protective, responsible mother. She attends the Steering School classes to determine what Garp should take, and she even chooses wrestling as his sport. Although she claims she is not a woman liberationist, she becomes one of the feminist movement's champions because of her book, *A Sexual Suspect*, the title and the opening sentences of which summarize her life: "I wanted a job and I wanted to live alone. . . . That made me a sexual suspect. . . . Then I wanted a baby. But I didn't want to have to share my body or my life to have one. . . . That made me a sexual suspect, too" (112). When she inherits her father's estate at Dog's Head Harbor, she turns it into a metaphorical nursing retreat for abused wives, lesbians, rape victims, and the Ellen Jamesians, a fanatic group of women extremists who have their tongues surgically removed to protest the rape of eleven-year-old Ellen James. Jenny's tireless devotion and energy will be her legacy to her family and friends:

> In Garp's opinion, his mother never stopped being a nurse. She had nursed him through the Steering School; she had been a plodding midwife to her own strange story; finally, she became a kind of nurse to women with problems. She became a figure of famous strength; women sought her advice. With the sudden success of *A Sexual Suspect*, Jenny Fields uncovered a

nation of women who faced making choices about how to live; these women felt encouraged by Jenny's own example of making unpopular decisions. (132–33)

In *Marriage*, Irving alludes to Severin's quasi-androgynous roles: he does most of the cooking, cares for the children, sleeps in Edith's gown "like a transvestite weight lifter" among the children, and his ambition is "to be a wife." In *Garp*, these allusions become reality when Robert Muldoon, a Philadelphia Eagle tight end, undergoes a sex-change operation and becomes Roberta Muldoon. In her attempts to reclassify herself, she is often confused about whether she should act like a man or a woman, a confusion underscoring the difficulties plaguing both men's and women's lives in the plot. She also teaches Garp to be more tolerant and compassionate toward women, especially the Ellen Jamesians. Garp becomes more sympathetic toward the woman's point of view when, at Roberta's insistence, he dresses as a woman to attend his mother's funeral. As Gabriel Miller points out, because Roberta is androgynous she becomes "almost a surrogate mother/father figure for Garp after Jenny's death" and a "mother/father" surrogate to Duncan after the car crash "when Garp and Helen are too sick and grief-stricken to be effective parents."[5] Nicknamed Captain Energy, Roberta, as does Jenny, tirelessly dedicates herself to the Fields Foundation, urges Garp to be its director so he would "understand the need" and "have to deal with the problems" (380), and she even nurses Duncan after his motorcycle accident. Moreover, Duncan is so impressed with Roberta's strength, compassion, and understanding that he marries a transvestite, "Another gift to Duncan's life from Roberta Muldoon"

(434). In interpreting this incident, Miller writes, "at least in the next generation, in life after Garp (and after Roberta) there is hope for real change, for true and lasting progress toward the goals of sexual transcendence and mutual understanding. This is perhaps Irving's most hopeful and life-affirming gesture in the novel."[6]

Bears, *Water-Method*, and *Marriage* analyzed the role of the family, but this theme comes to fruition in *Garp*. As Irving emphasizes, "I could not state a better or broader opinion of family life than is already written" in *Garp*.[7] Before he marries Helen, the family unit consisting of Jenny and Garp is closely knit. Jenny is ever watchful and dutiful about Garp's health and education, characteristics Garp will assume once he has his own family. Not only does Garp's and Helen's marriage unite two partial families, but their marriage is solidly based on their deepening love for each other:

> As it was, they were lucky. Many couples live together and discover they're not in love; some couples never discover it. Others marry, and news comes to them at awkward moments in their lives. In the case of Garp and Helen, they hardly knew each other but they had their hunches—and in their stubborn, deliberate ways they fell in love with each other after they were married. (130)

Because of this love and the love for children, the mate-swapping and Garp's and Helen's infidelities never destroy their marriage. Even though they lose Walt, their love deepens and transcends the tragedy. Garp is not unfaithful and even the "thought seldom occurred to him. . . . Enough of his life had been influenced by lust" (378), and after Garp's death, Helen confesses that he had "spoiled her . . . for even considering seriously the possibility of living with another man" (415). By extension, Jenny Fields's house becomes a surrogate family unit for society's cast-offs who need love and a sense of family togetherness.

In *Bears* and *Marriage*, rape symbolizes part of the terror and violence associated with the *Anschluss* and World War II, but except for Utch's mother, rape does not personally touch the characters' lives. Even though Garp alludes to the number of Viennese "babies born out of rapes," rape is a major theme, affects the main characters' lives, and is symptomatic of one evil lurking in the modern world. To quote Irving, rape "seems to represent the whole area of anarchy, chaos, viciousness, and amorality."[8] In *Garp*, for instance, the Ellen James plot reveals rape's viciousness. When she is eleven years old, Ellen James is raped by two men who cut out her tongue, but she writes out her rapers' descriptions, they are arrested, convicted, and eventually killed in prison. As a protest, the Ellen Jamesians have their tongues surgically removed. Although Garp has compassion for Ellen James, he is shocked with her "grown-up sour imitators" and their "*stupid* gestures" (137), which merely extend the rape's initial chaos. Garp also becomes involved with rape—"I feel uneasy . . . that my life has come in contact with so much rape" (148)—and he personally helps capture the Mustache Kid who raped a ten-year-old girl in the park. In addition, *The World According to Bensenhaver* is Garp's own novel about a violent rape and its even more violent aftermath. As he has done with mate-swapping in *Marriage*, Irving relentlessly analyzes the effects rape has on people's lives and exposes its vile ugliness, or as Irving says, rape is a "central crime. It's probably the most violent assault on the body and the head that can happen simultaneously—that doesn't kill you.''[9] Finally, rape will become a major theme in *Hotel New Hampshire* and a secondary theme in *Cider House*.

Irving also reintroduces a bear in ''The Pension Grillparzer,'' a narrative within *Garp*. Rather than representing unleashed forces as did the Asiatic Black Bear or cooperation as did the Rare Spectacled Bears in *Bears*, Duna has been declawed and trained to act like a human—he lives in the pension, uses the water closet, rides a unicycle, and wears the dream man's pin-striped suit. When Duna grows ''senile and indecent in its habits,'' he is donated to the Schonbrunn Zoo and dies two months later, ''his long history of having been treated as a human being did not prepare him for the gentler routine of zoo life'' (128). Although Miller sees Duna as symbolizing Austria's postwar ''limbolike existence,''[10] Duna cannot reassign itself to a bear's life just as the Pension Grillparzer cannot be reassigned a higher rating. The major characters, however, must always reclassify or reassign their priorities: Roberta must reassign her sexual role, Garp must reassign his ideas about women, especially the Ellen Jamesians, and he must realign his marriage after Helen's infidelity and the traumatic car crash. After Garp's death, Helen, Duncan, and Jenny Garp must constantly reclassify their goals, or their lives would be meaningless.

Garp effectively uses narratives-within-the narrative to illuminate incidents and themes. ''The Pension Grillparzer'' is about upgrading the pension from a C to a B rating, but because of its assortment of tenants, particularly the Circus Szlnok performers, the pension fails to be reclassified, a failure that emphasizes the failures that occur in Garp's world. "The Pension Grillparzer" is also about Vienna, death, and has an epilogue— similar techniques that appear in *Garp*. "Vigilance" is about Garp's mania for chasing down speeding cars in his neighborhood. But as he had successfully done with "The Pension Grillparzer," "Vigilance" is another attempt to court Helen because "Some instinct told him to court her again" (228). Garp senses that his marriage may be threatened, and indeed it is because of Helen's impending affair with Michael Milton, so indirectly both he and Helen must be vigilant in protecting and preserving their marriage.

The World According to Bensenhaver is about rape's vileness and the chaos that follows. Says Irving: rape "is a form of social violence, an extreme form, and it forces . . . a terrible reaction. The Bensenhaver story in *Garp* is simply the most brutal piece of documentary realism I can imagine on the subject."[11] In *Bensenhaver*, Oren Rath rapes Hope who kills Oren with his own knife while he is raping her; moreover, Arden Bensenhaver's young wife had also been raped and killed by three young boys in a laundromat. The chaos following Hope's rape occurs when her husband, Dorsey, hires Bensenhaver to protect his wife and family. Hope wants to have another child, but her rape has made Dorsey impotent and he suggests she be impregnated by her former lover. Obsessed by wishing to control the occasions when Hope is with her lover, Dorsey hides in Hope's closet on one occasion and is killed by Bensenhaver who eventually goes insane because of the amount of violence in his and other peoples' lives. Hope and her children, however, are unburdened from the terrible anxiety Dorsey created. In addition, within *Garp*, *Bensenhaver* voices Garp's own revulsion with Helen's affair and Walt's death, as well as his fears about his marriage's future. However, once he and Helen reconcile and Jenny is born, potential chaos gives way to love and strong family ties.

In *Garp*, Irving reintroduces wrestling and the wrestling room, and as metaphors, both elements augment plot and theme. Jenny goes to Seabrook Gymnasium and Field House to choose a sport for Garp because she believes men and women must have "muscles—to be strong." Once inside, Jenny senses "*competition*, fierce and full of disappointment" (54). After she chooses wrestling for Garp, the sport takes the "best of his energy until writing came along. He loved the singleness of the combat, and the frightening confines of that circle inscribed on the mat; the terrific conditioning; the mental constancy of keeping his weight down" (61). Wrestling will metaphorically prepare Garp for the exacting demands of his writing career, but more important, the sport will physically and mentally prepare him for contending with life's disappointments and tragedies, or simply life as fierce competition and often "full of disappointment."

Metaphorically, in *Garp* the wrestling room complements the paradoxical qualities of life. The room is a place of pain, and Jenny's first experiences involve a wrestler who is bleeding and vomiting, and the other wrestlers who are locked in "some violent tangle . . . as deliberate and as desperate as rape" (55). Juxtaposed with these violent images are the room's favorable associations. Jenny also feels "so *safe* here" because the room is "padded against pain" (60), and she and Ernie Holm realize that the wrestling room is "very safe for children—being padded everywhere and always warm" (57).

Within its womblike confines, Helen blossoms and matures, and Garp often takes his children there and rolls around on the mats with them because "sudden and inexplicable closeness is always possible" (59). Later, when Garp is almost killed by the Ellen Jamesian in the white Saab, Helen believes that Garp will be safe once the wrestling season begins, "Those warm mats and that padded room were a safety symbol to Helen Holm" (404). In accord with the novel's juxtaposition of comedy and tragedy, pain and even death resurface when Pooh Percy assassinates Garp in his beloved wrestling room.

A major symbol in *Garp* is the Under Toad. Repeatedly warned about the dangerous *undertow* at Dog's Head Harbor, Walt mistakenly translates the word into the Under Toad, a "giant toad, lurking offshore, waiting to suck him under and drag him out to sea" (341). Thereafter, for Garp and Helen, the Under Toad becomes "their code phrase for anxiety . . . as a way of referring to their sense of danger. When the traffic was heavy, when the road was icy—when depression had moved in overnight—they said to each other, 'The Under Toad is strong today' " (341). Whether Irving intends the Under Toad as an extension of the *Anschluss*-spawned violence is debatable, but the Under Toad certainly suggests the terrifying, enigmatic violence he attributes to the *Anschluss* in *Bears* and *Marriage*. Furthermore, a man who hates women kills Jenny, and a woman who hates men kills Garp; these assassins personify what Irving labels the "contemporary fascist spirit, a kind of born-again Nazism—this incredible self-importance, this incredible self-righteousness . . . to educate, to correct."[12] Irving will personify the "born-again Nazism" in the German radicals who terrorize the Berry family in *Hotel New Hampshire*. In addition, the

Under Toad recalls the "gale of the world" refrain in *Bears* and Sprog as a monstrous Devil's Toad in *Water-Method*.

The Under Toad also becomes the novel's major refrain and foreshadowing technique. As a foreshadowing, theUnder Toad imagery first appears when Stewart Percy and Harry are playing golf, and Harry hits a new golf ball onto a tidal flat. Harry wades into the muck and mires up to his waist: "An awful *slorp*ing noise pursued him through the mud flats, as if beneath the mud some mouth was gasping to suck him in" (73). Immediately before the crash in which Walt dies, Duncan describes the sensation of speeding down the dark driveway in the rain as "like being under water" (266)—the Under Toad's domain. Eventually the Under Toad surfaces as a full-fledged symbol and suggests ubiquitous, universal terror and death. On the flight to and during their stay in Vienna, for example, Garp senses the vile presence of the Under Toad. As he follows the landlady into the room to answer the phone call about his mother's murder, "Garp felt he followed the Angel of Death—midwife to the Under Toad whose swampy smell he sniffed at the mouthpiece of the phone. . . . The room reeked of toad" (345). At his mother's funeral, Pooh Percy recognizes Garp, and as she calls out his name, "The word *Garp* bounced like the burp of an unknown animal into the silence of the suffering auditorium" (359). When Ernie Holm dies and Garp enters the house, he hears the "cold hop of the Under Toad thudding across the cold floors of the silent house" (367). When Garp is almost killed by the Ellen Jamesian driving the white Saab, he hears the "croak of the vile-tasting Under Toad in his dry throat" (401). Moreover, the narrator ominously notes that Garp would "see the first edition of *The Pension Grillparzer*—illustrated by

Duncan Garp, and out in time for Christmas—before he saw the Under Toad'' (406). Finally, as he lies dying in the wrestling room, Garp recognizes that the Under Toad is neither a ''stranger'' nor is it ''mysterious'': ''It was yielding, like the warm wrestling mats; it smelled like the sweat of clean boys—and like Helen, the first and last woman Garp loved. The Under Toad, Garp knew now, could even look like a nurse: a person who is familiar with death and trained to make practical responses to pain'' (413).

Despite the ubiquitous Under Toad, *Garp* ends with a life-affirming epilogue. In Garp's world, an ''evening could be hilarious and the next morning could be murderous'' (406), but his quest is to live energetically and purposefully by embracing the positive qualities of life—humor, energy, responsibility, compassion, and love—and these virtues are defenses against the Under Toad. And as he lies mortally wounded in the wrestling room, he tries to convey these maxims to Helen:

> With his eyes, Garp tried to reassure her: don't worry—so what if there is no life after death. There is life after Garp, believe me. Even if there is only death after death . . . be grateful for small favors—sometimes there is birth after sex. . . . And if you are very fortunate, sometimes there is sex after birth. . . . And if you have life, said Garp's eyes, there is hope you'll have energy. . . . And never forget, there is memory. . . . And in the world according to Garp . . . we are obliged to remember everything. (413)

The ''small favors'' that are Garp's legacy become inspirations for other characters. Despite losing an eye and an arm, Duncan becomes a ''good and serious painter; he was something of a pioneer in the artistically suspect field of color photography, which he developed with a painter's eye for color and his father's habit of an insistent, *personal* vision'' (433). Jenny Garp tirelessly devotes herself to cancer research because she wishes to ''devote herself to something like the life Garp once described . . . 'trying to keep everyone alive, forever' '' (437). Before she dies, Roberta affirms, ''I want a *whole life* just like that one'' (430).

Even the fates of the other characters underscore the novel's affirmative vision. Dean Bodger remains loyal to Helen and to the Steering wrestling team. After rehabilitation therapy, Pooh Percy is ''peaceably reintroduced to social intercourse,'' becomes a devoted mother at fifty-four—''she got herself pregnant . . . (no one could imagine how)'' (422)—and works with retarded children. Florence Cochran Bowlsby, alias Mrs. Ralph, completes her Ph.D. in comparative literature and becomes a ''dynamite teacher'' (421). Ellen James becomes a ''good poet and ardent feminist who believed in living like Jenny Fields and believed in writing with the energy and personal vision of T. S. Garp'' (420). These positive, life-affirming images contrast with the cautious optimism evident at the end of *Bears*, *Water-Method*, and *Marriage* and thus emphasize Irving's more mature, optimistic world vision.

Bears and *Water-Method* combine the first- and third-person points of views, and *Marriage* uses the first-person narrator. *Garp*, however, uses the omniscient third-person narrator because, as Irving emphasizes, the plot needed a ''biographer's tone'' to depict Jenny Fields's and Garp's lives, and adds Irving: ''The practical reason for . . . the third person is that they are all terminal cases; they are all going to die. There is no storytelling. In other words, the last chapter is an obituary, and there's no one to tell the story if the story isn't in the third person.''[13]

Bears juxtaposed comedy with tragedy, *Water-Method* was pure comedy, and *Marriage* was more somber than comic. Originally titled *Lunacy and Sorrow*,[14] *Garp* balances comedy and tragedy. For example, a potentially tragic scene becomes comic when Dean Bodger catches a dead pigeon and mistakenly thinks he has saved Garp, whom he imagines has fallen from the infirmary roof. Some comical scenes ensue when Garp chases down neighborhood speeders, but one scene borders on tragedy when Garp so perturbs O. Fecteau, the plumber, who, in turn, tries to run down Garp and Roberta. Bonkers bites off Garp's ear, but potential horror gives way to comedy when Garp later retaliates and bites off Bonkers's ear, much to Fat Stewie's chagrin. The best example of the juxtaposition of comedy and tragedy occurs in the car crash when Helen bites off Michael Milton's penis; tragically Helen and Garp lose something far more precious, Walt. The novel's ultimate comedy results in the epilogue in which Irving assuages the violence and death at the novel's core.

Believing that Random House did not properly promote his first three novels, Irving switched publishers to E. P. Dutton primarily because of Henry Robbins, who, after reading the unfinished manuscript, recommended *Garp* for publication: ''A major novel about a wonderfully eccentric mother and son, very funny and very moving at the same time. Sure to be a 'breakthrough' by an immensely talented novelist in his mid-30s.''[15] Robbins also advanced Irving $20,000 and offered $150,000 on the next novel—''sight unseen.''[16] Moreover, Pocket Books allocated $200,000 to mass-market the paperback edition of

Garp, "Bus billboards, radio commercials, sweat-bands, and t-shirts announced 'I Believe in Garp.' "[17] *Garp* initially sold 120,000 hardback copies and over three million paperback copies, was on the *New York Times Book Review* best-seller list for twenty-five weeks, and won the National Book Award as the best paperback in 1979.

Garp was also critically acclaimed. Claiming that it was an "extraordinary work," R. Z. Sheppard wrote that with *Garp*, Irving "moves into the front ranks of America's young novelists."[18] While noting the murder, mayhem, and mutilations that dominate the plot, Eliot Fremont-Smith emphasized that the novel was about "how to breathe life into life" and how to "make things whole"; furthermore, Fremont-Smith praised the novel for the "wondrous mechanics of its invention and the deft manipulation . . . of our awe and tears and laughter."[19] According to Larry McCaffery, "Of all the novels to appear during the 1970s, *Garp* was probably the book which most captured the public's imagination. . . . Like Dickens and Günter Grass . . . Irving is a natural-born story teller who transcends the categories of 'academic' and 'popular' fiction writer."[20] In addition, Carol Harter and James Thompson wrote: "*The World According to Garp* unquestionably remains—both aesthetically and in terms of comprehensive appeal—Irving's most successful novel. . . . Intellectually and emotionally rich, complexly, yet lucidly structured and energetically written, it will remain . . . a major novel of the last years of this century."[21]

Despite such critical accolades, *Garp* has its detractors, or as Anne Tyler phrased it, the "Garp-haters."[22] In fact, while confirming that she was not an "Irving-hater" and admired his first three novels, Tyler admitted that she was a "Garp-hater": "I was put off by the book's casual cruelty, by its calculated, unwieldy plot and its staggering long-windedness. And . . . all those Garp T-shirts and blaring Garp book-dumps did seem excessive.''[23] Similarly, while admiring the novel's beginning—''a brief spring of enjoyment''—and Garp's Vienna sojourn with his mother—''the Indian summer of the book, before the darkness of boredom and the thunder of repellant acts set in''—Angela Huth wrote that once Garp marries ''clever, colourless Helen,'' the readers were ''in for a long spell of a dull American marriage which, in the hands less skilled than those of Updike or Heller, makes tedious reading.''[24] Bryan Griffin excoriated *Garp* for its plot—''Irving has never been able to construct a believable plot''; for its prose—Irving's ''vocabulary is uninspiring [and] his knowledge of grammatical proprieties is severely limited''; and for its lack of humor—''It tries to be. But it is low humor, based chiefly on the prepubescent assumption that conscientious vulgarity is by definition amusing.''[25]

Significantly, however, between *Bears* and *Garp*, Irving's writing skills matured, and *Garp* is certainly the best of the four novels. At the same time, *Garp* is a necessary bridge to *Hotel New Hampshire*, which Irving claims is even better: ''There's no question in my mind it's better than *The World According to Garp*. It certainly is every bit as big a book and it means much more. It's a more ambitious novel symbolically but with a different point of view, deliberately narrower than *Garp*.''[26]

NOTES

C1 1. Larry McCaffery, ''An Interview with John Irving,'' 8.

2. John Irving, *The World According to Garp*, 86; hereafter cited in the text.

3. Gabriel Miller, *John Irving*, 102.
4. McCaffery, "Interview," 8.
5. Miller, *John Irving*, 121.
6. *Ibid.*, 122.
7. Joyce Renwick, "John Irving: An Interview," 13.
8. Greil Marcus, "The World of *The World According to Garp*," 74.
9. *Ibid.*, 73.
10. Miller, *John Irving*, 104.
11. Laura de Coppet, "An Interview with John Irving," 42.
12. Miller, *John Irving*, 198.
13. de Coppet, "Interview," 44.
14. Miller, *John Irving*, 97.
15. R. Z. Sheppard, "Life into Art: Garp Creator Strikes Again," 51.
16. *Ibid.*
17. Richard West, "John Irving's World After *Garp*," 30.
18. R. Z. Sheppard, "Love, Art and the Last Puritan," *Time*, 111 (24 April 1978): 90–91.
19. Eliot Fremont-Smith, "Blood and Ketchup on the Mat," *Village Voice*, 22 May 1978: 78.
20. McCaffery, "Interview," 1.
21. Carol C. Harter and James R. Thompson, *John Irving*.
22. Anne Tyler, "*Three by Irving*," *The New Republic* 182 (26 April 1980): 32.
23. *Ibid.*
24. Angela Huth, "Rape Jape," *Listener*, (23 November 1978): 690.
25. Bryan Griffin, "Literary Hype" *Atlantic Monthly*, 243 (June 1979): 51, 55.
26. West, "Irving's World After *Garp*," 29.

CHAPTER SIX

"The Most Complete Unto Itself": *The Hotel New Hampshire* (1981)

Of his first five novels, Irving believes that *The Hotel New Hampshire* is "the most complete unto itself—that is, it is the most of itself an entered and then left world. You enter it and then you get out of it, and while you're in it, *its* rules apply, yours don't. To break that down a little . . . it's also the novel of mine that . . . requires the least amount of understanding of the so-called *real* and outside world."[1] Because *Hotel* is complete in itself, the settings are more related, the characters more interesting, and the themes and techniques more integrated and complex.

Hotel is primarily set in New Hampshire, New York, and Maine, but, as part of their initiation rites, the Berry family makes an obligatory trip to Vienna. In the other novels, the *Anschluss* and World War II mainly affect Vienna, but in *Hotel* Irving alludes to the effects of these events on the United States. John Berry, the narrator, suggests the pristine, almost magical quality of life in prewar America when he refers to that time as the "famous summer of the bear, and the magic of my mother's and father's courtship."[2] Even then are rumors of war, and when

Arbuthnot, proprietor of Arbuthnot-by-the-Sea, declares, "Europe's going to be no place for Jews" and the "world's going to be no place for bears" (14), he ominously predicts the Holocaust and the end of the old world. Inevitably war comes, and John Berry writes, "By the summer of 1942, the war had obtruded upon everyone; it was no longer just the 'war in Europe' " (35). Winslow Berry (AKA Father) is drafted, never enters combat, but the world to which he returns is changed nevertheless: "There were not many big bands around. Ballroom dancing was declining as a sport and pastime. And Earl was too decrepit to perform anymore" (37). The end of the old world symbolically occurs when the Berry family makes a nostalgic journey to the past and visits the deteriorating Arbuthnot-by-the-Sea. On the rotting pier, Earl, a performing bear that is also called State O'Maine, is killed by a young boy who symbolizes the postmodern world's sudden, absurd violence. Reflecting on his father's grief, John writes, "He was crying for more than Earl, of course. He was crying for the Arbuthnot, and Freud, and for the summer of '39" (40). The old world, both in the United States and Vienna, is gone, or as the children's mother says, "The war has changed a lot of things" (39).

In 1957 when the Berrys arrive in Vienna, the city reflects its war scars. They see "bombed-out buildings"; "rubbled lots" that may contain "unexploded bombs buried in the raked and orderly debris"; stone cupids with "their bellies pocked-marked by machine-gun fire"; a Russian tank "firmly arranged—in concrete—as a memorial"; and the city's outer districts resemble "old sepia photographs taken at a time of day before everybody was up or after everyone has been killed" (209). In addition,

Freud, Father's mentor from the Arbuthnot Inn, is another reminder of the *Anschluss*-spawned violence because he has been blinded in a Nazi death camp experiment. Furthermore, when Freud takes the children on tour, he invariably takes them to a dead past—to the memorial plaque on Franz Josef-kai that honors the Jews killed by the Gestapo; and to the Judenplatz, which in Freud's mind was still the 1939 Judenplatz; consequently, he identifies "apartments that were no longer apartments," entire "buildings that were no longer there," and the "*people* he used to know, they weren't there either" (260).

Under the innocuous title of the Symposium on East-West Relations, the young German radicals in the second Hotel New Hampshire are the afterbirth of evil spawned by the war. Having neither a sense of history nor a love for anything romantic, the radicals would destroy both the past and present in a holocaustic explosion. Using a contact bomb installed in an old Mercedes and a "sympathy bomb" under the stage, they plan to blow up the Vienna State Opera House because it represents an "institution that the Viennese worship to a *disgusting* extreme that they worship their coffeehouses—that they worship the past" (313). The terrorists' irrational, inhumane violence is apparent because they are "willing to murder and maim—not for a *cause*, which would be stupid enough, but for an *audience*" (314). These terrorists represent what Irving calls the "contemporary fascist spirit, a kind of born-again Nazism—this incredible self-importance, this incredible self-righteousness . . . to *educate*, to *correct*."[3] Moreover, when John Berry equates the terrorist with the pornographer—"The terrorist and the pornographer are in it *for* the means" (317)—he indirectly links their actions with one of the modern world's evils, rape, and specifically to Franny's and Susie the Bear's rapes, which are at the core of the novel. A rapist, moreover, terrorizes another person solely "*for* the means."

Unlike Trumper, Severin, and Garp, Win Berry is not an overly protective father mainly because he dreamily chases his illusions, which take shape in the three Hotel New Hampshires in the plot. He becomes a hero, however, when he kills Ernst, one of the terrorists, with a Louisville Slugger baseball bat. That he will not be a conventional father figure is emphasized when, after Mother's death, Franny says she will become a surrogate mother: " '*Father doesn't know what's going on*,' Franny said, and we nodded—Frank, Lilly, and I; even Susie the Bear nodded. We knew this was true: Father was blind, or he soon would be" (233). When Father is blinded, the children must take care of him as part of their initiation rites. Because he chases his dreams of the perfect hotel, Father's characterization is also pertinent to the plot's Gatsby allusions, and even Lilly exclaims, "It's the man in the white dinner jacket, it's Father, he's Gatsby. . . . There's always going to be an *It*. . . . It's going to *always* get away" (230). However, even though Father always pursues his illusions, his quest neither ends in tragedy like Gatsby's, nor does it end in bitterness and death as does Arbuthnot's, another figure in a white dinner jacket. Father's illusions instead become his reason for living fully, and they also become his children's quest, since all of them metaphorically become "caretakers" of their father's illusions. Finally, in emphasizing the positive qualities of dreams, the third Hotel New Hampshire is a successful rape crisis center, and John admits that his father's "illusions are powerful enough" to become "*his* good, smart bear—at last" (401).

The novel's narrator is John Berry who writes, "And so it's up to me—the middle child, and least opinionated—to set things straight, or almost straight" (1–2). In this light, not only must he adjust to and learn from the traumatic events of his life but he also becomes a Nick Carraway foil for his father's Gatsby-like characteristics. In addition, John's narration augments the bildungsroman theme and records the knowledge he and his family gain through experiences. Irving has commented that in *Hotel* he wanted to "keep the voice of [*The Pension Grillparzer*], a straight-forward first-person narrative told from a child's point of view that a child could understand. It would be a novel about growing up and how the impressions children have of themselves and those closest to them change as they grow older."[4] Consequently, John's narrative closely parallels the separation-initiation-return motif since he records their separation from the first Hotel New Hampshire, their further initiations in Vienna, and their return to the United States. Significantly, too, the novel's structure is circular—it begins and ends at Maine's Arbuthnot-by-the-Sea resort.

Franny Berry, the second oldest child, is the novel's foul-mouthed heroine, around whom the central actions swirl. She is gang raped on Halloween by Chipper Dove, Lenny Metz, and Chester Pulaski, three star players on Coach Iowa Bob's football team, and the rape is the children's first experience with violence. After Franny is raped, John becomes obsessed with weight lifting because he "never wanted to feel, again, the helplessness of another Halloween" (113). Franny, however, needs some sense of revenge to transcend the rape's ignominy. Fated justice befalls two of her attackers. Chester Pulaski dies in a car crash while fondling a girl instead of watching the road, and Lenny Metz cheats a Vietnam prostitute who poisons him. However, with the aid of Frank, Lilly, John, and Susie, Franny exacts her revenge on Chipper Dove by humiliating him in a scene that critics often fault but that Irving justifies:

> The whole point of it, and it says so in the book, is that revenge is a letdown, that it is finally an anticlimax. Whatever revenge was taken on Chipper Dove . . . would never be as awful as what he had done, and if it had been as awful, it would have been too much. . . . So all they do is scare him, because there's only two choices, scare him or kill him. Scaring him isn't good enough but it's as close as you can get.[5]

Because of the rape, Franny and John become aware of their love for each other and must somehow transcend this dilemma. They eventually make love so much that each physically hurts, and each realizes that incestuous love is self-defeating and life-negating: "Just imagine trying to live every day like this. . . . We'd go crazy," Franny said. "There's no living with this. . . . That's the end of it. Now we're free" (334). Once freed, Franny becomes a successful movie star and marries Junior Jones, who is a successful lawyer.

Frank, the eldest child, is a homosexual, and so he becomes an extreme example of Irving's androgynous males. Frank is also significant for the novel's life-affirming vision because he readily adjusts to his homosexuality, keeps "passing the open windows without the slightest trace of fear" (373), and becomes the family's businessman, Lilly's agent, and family hero, "He was a hero, but he needed to get to that point in time when he would be signing all our checks, and telling us how much we could spend on this or that, in order for us to recognize the hero that Frank had always been'' (376). Nevertheless, Lilly and Egg Berry are part of the family's tragedies. Less than four feet tall, dwarfish Lilly becomes a best-selling author when her *Trying to Grow* sells over 100,000 copies, is optioned as a movie, and then as a television series. Plagued by her mother's and Egg's death and by her obsession to grow as a writer, Lilly despairs and hurls herself out of her fourteenth-floor window in the Stanhope Hotel. Besides emphasizing the sudden deaths in the novel, Lilly's suicide ironically recalls one of the family's maxims—''Keep passing the open windows.'' Similar to Walt in *Garp*, Egg, as his name implies, is the child who will never grow up, and he and Mother are killed in the plane crash at sea. As part of the Berrys' initiation process, Egg's and Mother's deaths are personal tragedies that the Berrys must transcend.

To distinguish him from *the* Sigmund Freud, the Berry children always refer to Freud as ''our Freud.'' In addition to sealing the courtship and eventual marriage between Father and Mother (AKA Mary Bates), Freud underscores the violence terrorizing Vienna and the world before, during, and after World War II. To escape anti-Semitism in Europe, Freud comes to the United States, encounters more anti-Semitism from German tourists, and returns to Europe where he is blinded during an experiment in a Nazi concentration camp. Although he brags that ''Herr Todd [Mr. Death] never found me'' (259), he becomes a victim of ''born-again Nazism,'' the young German radicals. Freud's death, says Irving, is still heroic: ''I liked making him a hero. I liked letting him go out like a cowboy, because for all his family, for all the Jews in Europe, he is in a way making a gesture that many of his people were never given the opportunity to make. Not only did they have to die, but they couldn't bring a single villain down with them. So I really wanted to let him be the one who blows the bomb.''[6]

Instead of wrestling, weight lifting becomes the major sports metaphor in *Hotel* and prepares John physically and mentally for contending with life's tragedies. After Franny is raped and John wants to be stronger and protect her the next time, Iowa Bob encourages him to lift weights: ''You're the first member of this family who's taken a proper interest in his body. You've got to *get* obsessed and *stay* obsessed'' (111). After binge eating for bulk and jogging six miles a day plus running wind sprints, John weighs 150 pounds and is ''hard all over'' (111). When the German radicals threaten his family, John literally crushes Arbeiter to death:

> I imagined the biggest barbell in the world. I don't know exactly what I imagined I was doing with the barbell—curling it, bench-pressing it, dead-lifting it, or simply hugging it to my own chest. It didn't matter; I was just concentrating on its *weight* . . . I had been lifting weights since Franny was raped, since Iowa Bob showed me how; with Arbeiter in my arms, I was the strongest man in the world. (320)

Because he realizes his strength can be murderous, John says, ''I have never felt the same about weightlifting since. . . . A little light lifting, just enough to make me start feeling good; I don't like to strain, not anymore'' (321). Later when he meets Dove in New York and lifts him off the street, John simply puts him down, although he secretly feels like hugging Dove harder than he had hugged Arbeiter. As John says, ''There was really nothing to do with him except put him down; there never *would* be anything to do with him, too—with our Chipper Doves we just go on picking them up and putting them down, forever'' (360).

While in *Garp* the Under Toad symbolizes universal violence and death, the Berrys' Labrador retriever, appropriately and allegorically named Sorrow, symbolizes similar forces. Because of his age, halitosis, and interminable flatulence, Sorrow is mercifully put to sleep on Halloween, the night Howard Tuck dies of a heart attack and Franny is gang raped. As a biology project, Frank resurrects and stuffs Sorrow, first in an attack pose and then in a friendly pose—allegorically, then, as a fact of life, sorrow assumes many guises, especially death. For example, on Christmas Day as Iowa Bob and John lift weights, a weight slips off the bar, crashes into the closet door, and out glides Sorrow in his attack pose. Thinking Sorrow is going to attack, Iowa Bob dies of a heart attack when he hurls his body across John to protect him. That even Sorrow in a friendly pose—''I can make him nice again,'' says Frank (163)—will be frightening is implied when Franny warns, ''there was never any such thing as 'nice sorrow'; by definition, sorrow would never be nice'' (164). Later, when Mother and Egg die in the plane crash, the friendly posed Sorrow bobs to the ocean's surface to mark the site. Franny again warns the others, ''we must all watch out for whatever form Sorrow would take *next*; we must learn to recognize the different poses'' (206). As part of their initiation rites in Vienna, the Berrys experience other forms of sorrow. When he sees the radicals transporting the sympathy bomb, for instance, John remarks that it looks like a ''big dog. It was just a carload of sorrow'' (275); moreover, in the foiled bomb-plot sequence, sorrow becomes a reality when Freud is killed and flying glass shards blind Father. Sorrow also stalks the Berrys' lives in the United States when Lilly commits suicide: "She was the sorrow we never quite understood; we never saw through her disguises" (376).

Sorrow also indicates that Irving is more adept in developing his symbols. In accord with the bildungsroman motif, for instance, as the Berry children learn from their experiences, Sorrow's symbolic importance assumes added dimensions. While he is simply the family dog as the narrative opens, he changes from a symbol of violence and evil in the children's microcosm (e.g., Franny's rape; the deaths of Iowa Bob, Mother, and Egg) to a universal symbol of evil as emphasized by the lowercase *s* (e.g., Lilly "was the sorrow we never quite understood"; "Franny is skilled at keeping sorrow at bay").

Besides being a symbol, Sorrow becomes one of the novel's refrains. In the opening chapter, for example, John looks at Sorrow, imagines the dog changes shapes, and then says that "Sorrow could never be merely a dog" (4). Later, when Frank has stuffed Sorrow, Iowa Bob dreams that Sorrow wanted to kill him, and Frank ironically confides that Sorrow is "all ready . . . and he's coming home tonight" (135). From this point on, when Sorrow appears, either terror or death follows. When Bitty Tuck goes into Egg's bathroom to insert her diaphragm and sees the raggedy, singed Sorrow in the bathtub, she faints. In Vienna, Lilly's *Weltschmerz* translates into Sorrow: "Kind of like *sorrow*, huh, Frank?" asks Franny (230). The titles of Chapter Seven, "Sorrow Strikes Again," and Chapter Eight, "Sorrow Floats," emphasize the refrain and sorrow's role in life. In short, sorrow is part of and affects everyone's life, or as Frank says, "You can't kill it'' (247). In *Garp* the family must constantly beware of the Under Toad; in *Hotel*, the family must beware of Sorrow and recognize its different poses.

Another refrain is the Berrys' family maxim: ''Keep passing the open windows.'' According to Freud, the expression originated from a Viennese street clown, the King of Mice:

> HE TRAINED RODENTS, HE DID HOROSCOPES, HE COULD IMPERSONATE NAPOLEON, HE COULD MAKE DOGS FART ON COMMAND. ONE NIGHT HE JUMPED OUT HIS WINDOW WITH ALL HIS PETS IN A BOX. WRITTEN ON THE BOX WAS THIS: ''LIFE IS SERIOUS BUT ART IS FUN.'' (183)

The King of Mice's death, however, becomes a Viennese joke, or says Freud, ''WE SAY, 'KEEP PASSING THE OPEN WINDOWS.' THIS IS AN OLD JOKE'' (183). This refrain refers to life's capriciousness and emphasizes the determination to live purposefully and energetically despite what happens. For instance, Freud has endured one of life's most inhumane conditions in the Nazi death camp and refused to commit suicide. Furthermore, when Father talks with the rape victims at the third Hotel New Hampshire, his advice is always, ''Keep passing the open windows, my dear . . . That's the important thing'' (393). Despite universal sorrow and the very personal deaths of Iowa Bob, Mother, Egg, Freud, and Lilly, the surviving Berrys live happy, meaningful lives. They keep passing the open windows.

Another refrain in *Hotel* occurs when Iowa Bob tells John that if he wants to become strong he must ''*get* obsessed and *stay* obsessed.'' Through obsessive determination, John eventually becomes "hard all over," even though he admits that the "hard part, for most people, is the discipline" (113). Although Franny says she is dealing with her rape, Susie says, "You never got angry enough. You've got to get angry. You've got to get savage about all the facts," and to which Franks retorts, "You've got to get obsessed and stay obsessed" (216). In their lives, the surviving Berrys become obsessed with living well and happily, and the novel's concluding paragraphs provide their life-affirming dictums: "Coach Bob knew it all along. You've got to get obsessed and stay obsessed. You have to keep passing the open windows" (401).

As implied in the novel's title and the three Hotel New Hampshires in the plot, a major symbol is hotels. The Thompson Female Seminary is converted into the first Hotel New Hampshire in a difficult process that Iowa Bob humorously equates with "raping a rhinoceros" (64)—a remark juxtaposed with one of the novel's themes, rape's tragic consequences. To finance the first hotel, Mother must sell her father's house, and thus the Berrys become rootless and travel from hotel to hotel. In addition, as implied by the fourth floor's miniature sinks and toilets and since the Berry siblings are still children, the first hotel is a *microcosm*. This world is, furthermore, a bright, cheerful place through and around which the Berry children cavort, and in which Mother and Father make love. Yet, as part of their rites of passage, the children are initiated into death when Howard Tuck and Iowa Bob die, and into violence when Franny is gang raped.

By comparison, the second Hotel New Hampshire, the converted Gasthaus Freud, is drab, dark, and inhabited by metaphorical dark forces, the selfish prostitutes and the violent German radicals. Because it is in Vienna and greatly increases the children's experiences and knowledge, the second hotel is more of a *macrocosm*, and further emphasized by the prostitutes' polyglot names: Old Billig, Jolanta, Babette, Dark Inge, and Screaming Annie. The renovated Arbuthnot-by-the-Sea is the third Hotel New Hampshire, and the most symbolic of the three. According to Irving, the last hotel is "no hotel at all. . . . It is a place to get well again which is the process that has been going on throughout the novel."[7] In this sense, Frank and Franny often visit to renew themselves; Father's illusions are finally satisfied; the rape crisis center flourishes; and John and Susie await the birth of Franny's baby whom they will raise in this nurturing environment. As Father says, "A good hotel turns space and atmosphere into something generous, something sympathetic—a good hotel makes those gestures that are like touching you, or saying a kind word to you, just when (and *only* then) you need it. A good hotel is always there. . . . If you come to a great hotel in *parts*, in broken pieces . . . when you leave the great hotel you'll leave it *whole* again" (392, 393).

While bears had symbolic roles in *Bears* and *Garp*, in *Hotel* the two bears are both symbolic and actual characters. Earl is, first of all, a performing bear that belongs to Freud who sells him to Father. Earl, quite old when Father buys him, ages even more, begins to go blind, urinates or vomits in the sidecar, and after the war is "too decrepit to perform anymore" (37). When the Berrys visit the now closed, deteriorating Arbuthnot-by-the-Sea, Earl is shot by a young boy who thought he was a wild bear. According to Irving, "The bear called State O'Maine . . . is simply an emotional focus—someone who draws our sympathy. He's an innocent in the way human beings aren't innocent. . . . The plight of the bear is a summary in shorthand of the ruination and survival that's going on in the book as a whole."[8] In other words, the deteriorating Arbuthnot and the decrepit Earl are vestiges of the old world that are inevitably doomed by the *Anschluss* and World War II. As his father cradles Earl's head in his lap and weeps, John emphasizes the end of the old world: Father "was crying for more than Earl. . . . He was crying for the Arbuthnot, and Freud, and for the summer of '39" (40).

The second bear in *Hotel* is Susie the Bear, a girl dressed in a bear suit. Susie hides in her bear suit because she thinks she is ugly—"there's no discrimination quite like the Ugly Treatment" (219)—and because she was raped by two men who put a bag over her head—"I am the original not-bad-if-you-put-a-bag-over-her-head girl" (219). As Lilly Berry says: "You can make fun of Susie because she's afraid to simply be a human being and have to *deal* . . . with other human beings. But how many human beings feel that way and don't have the imagination to do anything about it? It may be stupid going through life as a bear . . . but . . . it takes imagination" (263). Her bear suit is a defense against the world's violence, and it is her way of controlling violence: "I'm really not so tough, but no one tries to fight a bear. All I have to do is grab someone and they roll into a ball and start moaning. . . . No one fights back if you're a bear" (220). Irving says that Susie the Bear is "no real bear, it's the bear in us, or something."[9] In this light, Susie symbolizes the bearish tenacity she uses to contend with her rape and with life's overwhelming forces. In reflecting on her rape, for instance, John concludes, "This kind of cruelty might make a bear out of anyone" (307), and later, when he realizes he loves her, he says it is because of "her bearishness, for her complicated courage" (388). Similarly, in protecting his family from the German radicals' cruelty, John squeezes Arbeiter to death in a bear hug. In the face of sorrow, violence, and death, the Berrys are obsessed with a bearish tenacity to survive and each has a symbolic bear: "Frank has a good, smart bear for a mind. And Franny has a good, smart bear named Junior Jones. . . . My father's illusions are *his* good, smart bear. . . . And that leaves me with Susie the Bear . . . so I'm all right too" (401).

As do the preceding novels, *Hotel* ends with a life-affirming epilogue. However, unlike *Garp*, in which everyone dies, the Berrys continue living. Franny is a successful movie starlet, Frank is a successful businessman, Father lifts weights and enjoys the third hotel, and John marries Susie. Despite sorrow, violence, and death, they survive by adhering to another family dictum:

> The way the world worked was *not* cause for some sort of blanket cynicism or sophomoric despair; according to my father and Iowa Bob, the way the world worked—which was badly—was just a strong incentive to live purposefully, and be determined about living well. . . . Thus the family maxim was that an unhappy ending did not undermine a rich and energetic life. This was based on the belief that there *were* no happy endings. (149–50)

Thus each Berry has a "good, smart bear," each one becomes obsessed and stays obsessed with living energetically and purposefully, and each one keeps passing the open windows. And as John writes, "In the Hotel New Hampshire we're screwed down for life—but what's a little air in the pipes, or even a lot of shit in the hair, if you have good memories'' (400).

As was *Garp*, *Hotel New Hampshire* became another commercial success. E. P. Dutton initially published 175,000 copies and followed with a second printing of 100,000 copies; Pocket Books paid $2.3 million for the paperback reprint rights; and the Book-of-the-Month Club chose *Hotel New Hampshire* as its November selection.[10] At the same time, reviewers and critics were more divided regarding the novel's merits. After noting that the novel has the ''Irving benchmarks . . . body-building, bears, Viennese whores, rape and the pleasures of sexual intercourse,'' Robertson Davies writes, ''It would be unjust to call this 'the mixture as before,' because it is fresh and newly invented.''[11] Nancy Walker also notes that *Hotel New Hampshire* relies on previous Irvingesque ''themes and motifs,'' but its tone is ''more assured, its humor more sophisticated, its presentation of life more realistic than in much of Irving's other work.''[12] Eliot Fremont-Smith enthusiastically endorses *Hotel New Hampshire*: ''It's sheer energy all the way, plus magnetic characters, scenic wonders, horrendous happenings, and raffish, boffo jokes on every page. It warms the mind, tickles the funnybone, squeezes the heart; it alerts concern, then punctures it with a fart, followed by a hug. This book loves us.''[13]

On the other hand, while they say the novel suffers from being too long, from ''some silliness that is meant to be more like 'the stirring instabilities of American humor' found in *Garp*,'' and from its inability to ''imbue [its] fantasy world with profundity,'' Carol Harter and James Thompson conclude that *Hotel New Hampshire* is an ''interesting experiment'' in rediscovering new uses for romance that it honors and imitates.[14] Scott Haller argues that *Hotel New Hampshire* is not Irving's "best novel": "It lacks the urgency of *Setting Free the Bears*, the bittersweet wit of *The 158-Pound Marriage*, the sly set-ups of *Garp*."[15] Robert Towers claims that the language in *Hotel New Hampshire* lacks the "confidence, the aphoristic precision, and the vivacity that are among the pleasures of [*Garp*]," and that Irving hides these stylistic deficiencies with "literary crutches, quoting at length from the poems of Donald Justice and from the famous conclusion of *The Great Gatsby*."[16] Although praising Irving for his storytelling abilities—"he can keep as many narrative balls in the air without dropping them as anyone in America now writing fiction"—Gene Lyons found *Hotel New Hampshire* "not only a confusing but a boring novel" because it "declines into mere Creative Writing. . . . Creative Writers don't write about anything. . . . They wax creative."[17]

While its strengths and weaknesses are equally arguable, *Hotel New Hampshire* indicates Irving's maturing literary talents. The first-person narration is chronological and thus easier to read than the convoluted plot shiftings and points of view in *Bears* and *Water-Method*. Moreover, the narrative line in *Hotel New Hampshire* is not interrupted by stories-within-stories, a technique that proved disconcerting to some readers of *Garp*. Irving is also more adept in developing his symbols and metaphors, both of which, in accord with the bildungsroman motif, assume added dimensions and meanings as the Berry children learn from their experiences. Sorrow, for example, is simply the family dog as the narration opens, but then he changes from a symbol of evil in the children's microcosm (Franny's rape; the deaths of Iowa Bob, Mother, and Egg) to a universal symbol of evil as emphasized by the lower case "s" (Lilly "was the sorrow we never quite understood"; "Franny is skilled at keeping sorrow at bay"). Likewise, the metaphorical significance of the three Hotel New Hampshires changes as the children mature, or to quote Irving:

> The first hotel is the only real hotel in the story. It is childhood. The one in Vienna is a dark, foreign place, that phrase called adolescence, when you begin leaving the house and finding out how frightening the world is. . . . I wanted it morally, philosophically, politically, and sexually foreign and strange. . . . The last one is no hotel at all. . . . It is a place to get well again.[18]

In *Bears*, Irving experimented with convoluted plots; in *Water-Method*, with shifting points of view; in *Garp*, with narratives within the main narrative. In *Hotel New Hampshire*, he experiments with the fairy tale: "It has the completeness of 'Once upon a time . . . ' fairy tale," says Irving.[19] The fairy-tale framework coincides with John Berry's first-person narration in that his wistfully nostalgic language will recall the "famous summer of the bear, and the magic of my mother and father's courtship" (2). And there are fairy-tale characters: a wizard (Freud); a talisman (the man in the white dinner jacket); animals (Sorrow, State O'Maine, Susie the Bear); evil forces (Chipper Dove and the German radicals); a quest (to live "purposefully" and "well"); and heroes (the Berry family). Yet, the novel is also about rape, incest, homosexuality, lesbianism, violence, and death. While the Berrys hope for a fairy-tale existence, these forces shatter their dreams. Nevertheless, as John wistfully emphasizes in the conclusion: "But we dream on, and our dreams escape us almost as we can imagine them. That's what happens, like it or not. And because that's what happens, this is what we need: we need a good, smart bear'' (401). The novel has begun with a story about a fairy-tale hotel and a bear. It ends with a bear at a fairy-tale hotel.

Irving has always been praised for his inventive literary techniques and for dealing with major contemporary issues. In this light, each of his novels marks a definite progression from its predecessor. Irving continues this progression with his next novel, *The Cider House Rules*.

NOTES

1. Gabriel Miller, *John Irving*, 193.
2. John Irving, *The Hotel New Hampshire*, 2; hereafter cited in the text.
3. Miller, *John Irving*, 198.
4. Richard West, ''John Irving's World After *Garp*,'' 30.
5. Laura de Coppet, ''An Interview with John Irving,'' 44.
6. *Ibid.*
7. West, ''Irving's World After *Garp*,'' 31.
8. de Coppet, ''Interview,'' 42.
9. Miller, *John Irving*, 195.
10. R. Z. Sheppard, ''Life into Art: Garp Creator Strikes Again,'' 46.
11. Robertson Davies, ''John Irving and His Traveling Menagerie,'' *Book World, Washington Post*, 6 September 1981, 1.
12. Nancy Walker, ''John Irving,'' 1423.
13. Eliot Fremont-Smith, ''Floating Irving,'' *Village Voice*, 26. 35 (26 August–1 September, 1981): 35.
14. Carol C. Harter and James R. Thompson, *John Irving*, 125.
15. Scott Haller, ''John Irving's Bizarre World,'' 31.
16. Robert Towers, ''Reservations,'' *New York Review of Books*, 28(5 November 1981): 14–15.
17. Gene Lyons, ''Something New in Theme Parks,'' *The Nation*, 233 (26 September 1981): 278.
18. West, ''Irving's World After Garp,'' 31.
19. Larry McCaffery, ''An Interview with John Irving,'' 17.

CHAPTER SEVEN

"You Don't Compare Your Children": *The Cider House Rules* (1985)

Regarding *The Cider House Rules*, Irving admits, "I feel very comfortable about this book—more so than my other five books," but he refuses to compare his works: "You don't compare your children, really. You have to love each one."[1] Yet, major differences between his former novels and *Cider House*, become evident, especially in its settings, characterizations, themes, and techniques.

Noticeably absent in *Cider House* are Vienna and the emphasis on the *Anschluss* and its aftermath. World War II does indirectly intrude on the characters' lives—gas rationing and blackouts are in effect; Homer and Candy are volunteers in a veterans' hospital; and Ray Kendall and Melony work in navy shipyards. The war intrudes most traumatically when Wally Worthington's B-24 bomber is shot down over Burma, and he is an MIA for almost a year as Burmese guerrillas smuggle him through jungles to allied lines. Even then, the Burmese setting does not dominate a major portion of the narrative as did Vienna and the *Anschluss* in Irving's preceding novels. If anything, as suggested by the characters' rather routine lives in the United States and by Wally's bombing missions at altitudes from fourteen to fifteen thousand feet, the war's fury is remote. Even Wally and his crew members do not die in the plane crash nor on their journeys to allied lines.

In addition, for an Irving novel, the United States setting is more limited and focuses on three small Maine towns, St. Cloud's, Heart's Rock, and Heart's Haven. Located on an inland river, St. Cloud's had been a booming logging town founded by the Ramses Paper Company, but after denuding the forests—symbolically raping the land—without planting new trees, the company closes the town and moves downstream. Left behind are the buildings, the sawdust, the "scarred, bruised" river bank, the "less attractive prostitutes, and the children of these prostitutes."[2] Because of its location, St. Cloud's is usually swathed in clouds; fog hovers over the river until midmorning; and the waterfalls produce a constant mist. In addition, summers are stiflingly hot; fall is "five minutes long"; winters are snowed in; and spring brings "thawing mud." St. Cloud's dark, brooding, and melancholic atmosphere isolates the orphanage in which Dr. Wilbur Larch delivers or aborts babies.

In contrast, Heart's Rock, the site of the Worthingtons' Ocean View Orchards, and Heart's Haven, the site of Ray Kendall's dock and lobster pounds, are bathed in sunshine, refreshed by ocean breezes, and thickly populated. Whereas at St. Cloud's the birth processes are either terminated or produce an unwanted baby, the orchard's business is growing apples that are always needed and used, and Ray's business is producing more lobsters and repairing machinery. Major contrasts between St. Cloud's and the seacoast towns become apparent when Candy Kendall and Wally Worthington arrive in St. Cloud's in the oyster-white Cadillac with its "gold monogram on the face of a gleaming Red Delicious apple—with a leaf of spring-green brightness" (181). With their blond hair, suntans, pleasant personalities, and affluent airs, Wally and Candy awe everyone from the stationmaster to Mrs. Grogan, Larch, Homer, and especially the orphans who think this "lovely couple" wishes to adopt one of them. With their promises of "spring-green brightness," these light images are juxtaposed with the orphanage's old buildings, the dour women coming for abortions, and the brooding atmosphere of St. Cloud's. When Homer leaves with Candy and Wally, he leaves St. Cloud's dark atmosphere for Heart's Rock and the promise of sunlight, ocean breezes, friendship, and love.

Irving admits that in *Cider House* he "sets atmosphere and creates a landscape,"[3] and this is Irving's first novel in which he establishes landscapes with dark and light images. These images do not suggest, however, evil and good. For example, while St. Cloud's location and weather may suggest Larch's illegal abortions, the orphanage is a haven for unwanted babies who are loved, nurtured, and eventually adopted. In addition, when Homer and Candy return to have their son Angel, "they enjoyed the life of a young married couple that winter in St. Cloud's" (399). Angel not only symbolizes love and promise, but the apple trees Homer plants during their stay suggest a hopeful future for the orphanage. Although Heart's Rock and Heart's Haven suggest sun, sea, and promise, both towns will be affected by social discord, death, and World War II: "But trouble can come to nice places, too; trouble travels; trouble visits" (139). Significantly, too, though Homer's love is strengthened at Heart's Rock, this is only a temporary haven until he returns to assume Larch's duties. What Irving ultimately suggests in the landscape's light and dark images is the shifting reality that governs the nature of life, love, duty, responsibility, and rules.

Dr. Larch is one of the novel's protagonists. Before Larch goes to medical school, his father buys him the only present he has ever given his son, Mrs. Eames, a Portland whore from whom Larch contracts gonorrhea. To endure the pain from this venereal disease, Larch becomes addicted to ether, an indulgence that will last a lifetime and will finally kill him. His venereal disease, his attempts to save Mrs. Eames and her daughter, and his aborting Missy Channing-Peabody's baby convince Larch that he should remain celibate, return to Maine to deliver either mothers or babies, and establish an orphanage. Not only does he become a father figure for Homer Wells, whom he grooms and educates to take his place, but Larch also becomes a father figure for the other orphans, and after Homer leaves for Ocean View, Larch kisses all the boys goodnight. In a quasi-religious sense, Larch assumes a saintly, if not godlike, stature and is often referred to as St. Larch. As instances, he chooses celibacy; he lives among the clouds and mists of St. Cloud's; and he writes his chronicles that suggest gospels according to St. Larch. Furthermore, Larch's characterization is an integral part of the novel's abortion theme, the affirmative ending, and the *rules* metaphor.

Irving remarked that for *Cider House* he "wanted to write an orphan novel" because orphans are a universal subject and a "rich territory."[4] Among Irving's characters, Homer Wells, the other protagonist, is Irving's first true orphan who does not know who his father or mother is. Although Homer is adopted by several families, various circumstances intervene, and he returns to St.

Cloud's. For instance, the second foster family abuses Homer and Larch rescues him; the Drapers are religious fanatics whose grandson tries to "bugger Homer" (31), and Homer hitchhikes back to St. Cloud's; and when the Winkles are crushed to death in a river log jam, Homer flees to the safety of St. Cloud's. Unadoptable, Homer is unofficially adopted by Larch, his surrogate father. Although the novel traces several characters' lives from youth to middle age, Homer's life is the central bildungsroman. Homer also becomes embroiled in the novel's major conflict regarding choices and abortion. When he finds the aborted fetus near the incinerator and decides that it had been a living soul, he chooses not to perform abortions and thus conflicts with Larch's philosophy. While the conflict between Larch and Homer becomes the central plot line, it also eventually underscores the *rules* metaphor in the novel's title. As part of his rites of passage, Homer will see that, while rules keep people from being hurt, rules are often bent or changed.

Unlike Irving's other novels, *Cider House* focuses on two protagonists. While Homer grows up, the first five chapters treat Dr. Larch's life before and after he flees Boston for St. Cloud's. As Larch grows older, the last six chapters examine Homer's life after he flees St. Cloud's for Heart's Rock. Technically, this shifting of the focus from Larch to Homer also coincides with the developing conflict between them regarding abortions. This conflict is resolved in the novel's epilogue and is complemented by the novel's circular structure since the narrative begins and ends at St. Cloud's, and both Larch and Homer have fled the outside world for St. Cloud's.

Candy Kendall also becomes an integral part of the novel's themes and metaphors. As was Helen Holm in *Garp*, Candy is a semi-orphan, since her mother dies when Candy is very young and her father raises her. Since the novel traces her life from youth to maturity, she is also indigenous to the bildungsroman motif. In terms of the abortion theme, she first chooses to abort Wally's baby for an insignificant reason—"having to get married ahead of schedule" (150)—but she chooses to have Homer's child. Her choices emphasize one of Larch's arguments: a woman must have a choice; furthermore, her choices complement the *rules* metaphor and the idea that choices and rules are often changed. Her characterization entails one of the novel's most complex themes, love. Initially, she loves and is loyal to Wally, and, although attracted to Homer, she does not "encourage him" because she is "keeping her promise, about waiting and seeing" (349). When Wally has been presumably killed over Burma, Candy and Homer do not wait and see and consummate their love. When Wally returns, a love-triangle results, but unlike the mate swapping and infidelities in *Garp* and *Marriage*, no tragedy ensues nor do the three become estranged. Although she loves Wally and Homer equally, she eventually decides to marry Wally and care for him, a fortuitous decision that sends Homer back to St. Cloud's. Indeed, Candy's role suggests love's complicated nature that, like rules and choices, often shades from light and dark to gray, or as Rose Rose tells Angel, "Lovin' someone don't always make no difference" (540). Like Irving's other heroines, Candy typifies the independent woman and the dutiful, loving wife and mother.

Wally Worthington is significant for the novel's themes and metaphors. With his blond hair, suntan, affable personality, and hero's body, he personifies the light imagery and hope-for-the-future theme. Indeed, his jovial, loving personality never alters regardless of what befalls him.

Wally also typifies the war's effects on people's lives, and, when his plane, ironically named *Opportunity Knocks*, is shot down, Homer and Candy now have the opportunity to consummate their love. Within the love triangle, Wally assumes a neutral position in that he constantly urges Homer and Candy to look after each other when he is away at college or war. His neutral position is even more apparent when he becomes impotent as a result of his Burmese sojourn. Or, as Wally jokes with Homer, "I can still aim the gun, and the gun still goes off . . . with a bang. . . . It's just that no one ever finds the bullet" (450). Although when he returns home and knows that Homer and Candy are in love and that Angel is their child, Wally waits to see whom Candy will choose. Nevertheless, he always says that he loves them all, and thus his selfless love becomes a stabilizing, sturdy influence in their lives, a metaphorical heart's rock, or, as Ray Kendall emphasizes, "anyone could see the boy was good-hearted" (146).

As an orphan and part of the bildungsroman theme, Melony's life is detailed from childhood to death. She had been left at the orphanage when she was four or five, was big for her age, had not talked until she was eight or nine because she was "always angry," and had been "adopted and had been returned more times than Homer" (89). Her destructive anger is apparent in the scene in which she devastates the abandoned lumber company bunkroom, and in the number of brawls she has, especially with men who try to take advantage of her. As Harter and Thompson note, she also initiates Homer in sexual matters: "If Larch instructs Homer in 'the products of conception,' Melony teaches him all about the process."[5] In her own way, she loves Homer, whom she lovingly nicknames Sunshine, and when Homer goes with Candy and Wally, Melony leaves St. Cloud's to search for Homer. In this sense, she typifies one of the many instances of unrequited love in the plot—for instance, Candy's and Homer's love, Nurse Edna's love for Larch, and Angel's love for Rose Rose. Or, once again, "Lovin' someone don't always make no difference" (540). When Melony finally finds Homer and immediately recognizes Angel's parentage, she reinforces Homer's own dark thoughts about his immoral affair with Candy: "I somehow thought you'd end up doin' somethin' better than ballin' a poor cripple's wife and pretendin' your own child ain't your own. . . . You of all people—you, an orphan. . . . It's ordinary, middle-class shit—bein' unfaithful and lyin' to kids" (469). Melony also figures prominently in the novel's affirmative vision in that she adjusts to her life with Lorna, tempers her anger, and finally becomes "relatively happy" and "relaxed" (551).

Unlike Irving's previous novels in which the family formed a protective nucleus, external forces fracture the various families in *Cider House*. Wallace Senior's death fractures the Worthington family; Candy's mother dies; and the black migrant workers' family lives are rootless. While the potential for forming a family unit between Wally and Candy is fractured by the war, the only other possible chance for a strong family unit would be between Homer, Candy, and Angel, but that opportunity is fractured when Wally returns home. Within the novel's plot, however, the fractured families invariably form units as protection against life's tragedies. The orphanage, of course, has a father image in Larch, and four mother images in Mrs. Grogan and nurses Edna, Angela, and Caroline, all of whom nurture and protect the orphans. Olive

Worthington and Ray Kendall become surrogate mother and father images for Candy, Homer, and Wally, and like worried parents, Olive and Ray are concerned but understanding about Homer's and Candy's affair. Despite its complications, the Homer-Candy-Wally triangle also forms a family unit since all three of them love Angel and even protect Rose Rose from her father. Despite its turbulent periods, Melony and Lorna form a family unit based on protection and love. The positive, life-affirming values of these family units contrast with the life-negating qualities of other families in the novel—for example, the Lithuanian family, Mrs. Eames and her daughter, and even the Channing-Peabody family. The most tragic example of a fractured family occurs when Mr. Rose abuses and impregnates Rose Rose who, after her abortion, fatally stabs her father, flees with her first baby, and becomes rootless, or as Muddy says, "She don't know where she goin'. . . . She just know she gotta go" (541).

No symbols of violence and death similar to the Under Toad or Sorrow stalk the characters' lives in *Cider House*. Deaths there are, but they are less spectacular than those in the other novels. Wallace Worthington, Sr., dies of Alzheimer's disease, and Olive dies from cancer before Wally returns from the war. The bizarre deaths are also less spectacular. The stationmaster dies of fright when he sees Larch's and Homer's colossal shadows on the nightscape; Ray Kendall is blown to bits by his homemade torpedo; Melony dies in an electrical accident at the shipyards; Mr. Rose quietly bleeds to death after Rose Rose stabs him; and Larch dies from an ether overdose. However, when women attempt to terminate their pregnancies or visit charlatan abortionists, the results are violent and deadly. Mrs. Eames, for example, tries to abort herself by taking large quantities of the French Lunar Solution, an oil of tansy that rots her uterus. Mrs. Eames's daughter, who could not pay the abortion fee, is beaten by unknown assailants about her face and neck, her underwear is pinned to her shoulder, and she dies: "The hemorrhage and infection could have come from any of the several methods employed 'Off Harrison' " (60), the location of an illegal abortion clinic. The suggested overtones of violence and death in these incidents emphasize Larch's pro-choice stance and the medically safe abortions he performs.

Although abortion is a major theme in *Cider House*, Irving emphasizes: "I wanted to write an orphan novel. It was a year before abortion entered the story. But it made perfect sense. In the early part of the century, what doctor would be most sympathetic to performing abortions but a doctor who delivered unwanted babies, then cared for them in an orphanage?"[6] Claiming that he neither knew abortion would be a major emphasis in the novel nor that he knew *Cider House* would be published when abortion would become a crucial, national issue, Irving says: "A novelist is like a horse with blinders on. . . . But I'd really be wearing a false coat if I pretended that the real reason abortion is such an issue in the novel is that it makes a better story. I was happy to use it."[7]

In *Cider House*, Irving details the history of various abortion methods, legal and illegal, as well as some of the unsavory details of botched, often fatal, attempts. But he also compassionately depicts the pregnant women's suffering, humiliation, and guilt. When they arrive, "Several of the women had their faces in their hands, or sat as stonily as the other kind of mourner at a funeral—the one who must assume an attitude of total disinterest or else risk total loss of control''; and when they leave, ''Homer knew they did not look delivered of *all* their problems when they left. No one he had seen looked more miserable than these women; he suspected it was no accident that they left in darkness'' (30). Moreover, one of the many gospels according to St. Larch advocates understanding and sympathy for such women. For example, he tells Missy Channing-Peabody's boyfriend-seducer to ''treat her like a princess. . . . No one should be allowed to make her feel ashamed'' (74).

Irving also suggests the complicated nuances of the pro-life, pro-choice issues. While these nuances are evident in the central conflict between Larch and Homer regarding abortions, they are also evident in Candy's less pressing decision to abort Wally's baby because it means getting married ahead of schedule, and in the more pressing decision to abort Rose Rose, who had been impregnated by her own father. As Homer aborts Rose Rose and returns to St. Cloud's, the denouement favors pro-choice, but the novel's details affirm neither pro-choice nor pro-life. Instead, Irving only reveals nuances that, like the landscape, shift from dark and light to gray. As Benjamin DeMott notes: ''Responsive to the ideals and passion that drive both parties—pro-life, pro-choice—the author does not tease himself with delusions that a sunny negotiated accord waits just down the road. . . . Mr. Irving draws the readers close, in the space of his imagination, to an understanding of essential links, commonalities—even unities—between factions now seething with hatred for each other.''[8]

The novel is also about civic laws and personal rules that govern people's lives and actions. Often circumstances demand that certain laws must be broken and certain rules must be changed. As Wally tells Angel: "Some rules are good. . . . But some rules are just rules. You just got to break them carefully" (441). As its title suggests, a controlling metaphor in *Cider House* is rules, especially as they relate to abortion. In the novel's historical background, abortion is illegal. However, because of his experiences at the Boston Lying-In hospital, at the illegal abortion clinic "Off Harrison," at the Channing-Peabody estate, and with Mrs. Eames and her daughter, Dr. Larch develops his own pro-choice rules:

> He was an obstetrician; he delivered babies into the world. His colleagues called this "the Lord's work." And he was an abortionist; he delivered mothers, too. His colleagues called this "the Devil's work," but it was *all* the Lord's work to Wilbur Larch. As Mrs. Maxwell had observed: "The true physician's soul cannot be too broad and gentle." (75)

Larch also creates his own guidelines as he chronicles the history of the orphanage, and these rules always benefit the orphans. Homer Wells also develops his personal code of conduct about abortion and realizes, "If Larch has a choice, I have a choice, too" (169). Larch even acknowledges Homer's right to choose: "Well, I've never forced you. . . . And I never will. It's all your choice" (172).

Even in Heart's Haven and Heart's Rock are rules. When Candy is pregnant, she and Wally could easily marry, but because they are "simply stunned at the prospect of having to derail their perfect plans" (150), they change the rules. Homer encounters unwritten courtship rules when he takes Debra Pettigrew to the drive-in movies: "In Maine, in 194_, Homer Wells was forced to accept that what they called 'necking' was permitted; what they called 'making out' was within the rules'' (289). Yet, as Homer also realizes, sex is against the rules unless people are in love: ''So those are the rules! It's about accidents, it's about getting pregnant and not wanting to have a baby. My God, is everything about that?'' (290). Rules are also tacked over the light switch in Ocean View's cider house, but, except for Mr. Rose, none of the black workers can read and so never follow the rules. Yet, the blacks have rules governing their lives in the cider house—''The *real* cider house rules were Mr. Rose's'' (362).

These separate rules for the workers suggest that when rules clash, some of them are broken, and numerous rules are broken in the novel. Larch and his staff violate laws by performing abortions. Homer and Candy break moral rules when they begin their affair and continue it after Wally returns home. Indeed, Mr. Rose emphasizes these broken rules when he hands Homer the candle stub he and Candy use for their clandestine trysts in the cider house and says, ''That 'gainst the rules, ain't it?'' (519). Mr. Rose breaks a rule when he has sex with Rose Rose, and Homer breaks his rule when he aborts Rose Rose's baby and returns to St. Cloud's to continue Larch's work. As he does with the abortion issues, Irving suggests the complicated nature of rule-making and rule-breaking, which is never a question of light or dark, right or wrong, but rather of shaded nuances:

> And what were the rules of St. Cloud's? What were Larch's rules? Which rules did Dr. Larch observe, which ones did he break, or replace—and with what confidence? Clearly Candy was observing some rules, but whose? And did Wally know what the rules were?

> And Melony—did Melony obey any rules? Homer wondered. (362)

One major refrain in *Cider House* is the expression "wait and see." Initially, it refers to the inescapable love affair between Candy and Homer. After admitting their love for each other, Candy cautions Homer, "You have to wait and see. . . . For everything—you have to wait and see" (341). After he joins the Army Air Corps, Wally asks Candy to marry him, but she refuses and later explains to Homer, "For years I've expected to be married to Wally. You came along second. I have to wait and see about you. And now comes the war. I have to wait and see about the war, too" (347). When Wally is missing in Burma, however, Homer and Candy do not wait, and Candy gets pregnant, which entails more waiting and seeing. When Wally will return home, Candy must wait and see how she feels about him. In fact, all of the characters' lives and actions hinge on waiting and seeing. The pregnant women wait for abortions or deliveries; Olive waits for Wally's return; Ray Kendall knows he has "to wait for something to break before he can fix it" (341), a symbolic reference to Candy's affair with Homer; Angel must wait to see who his parents are; even growing apples is a wait-and-see process. Larch, however, never waits, and he begins his elaborate scheme to change Homer's identity to Dr. Stone. Tiring of waiting and seeing, Homer finally tells Candy that they must eventually tell Angel who his parents are. Generally, the wait-and-see refrain suggests that there are times in life for waiting, but there are also times for acting.

The second major refrain, and the title of the third chapter, occurs when Larch or Homer finishes the nightly readings and says, "Good night—you Princes of Maine, you Kings of New England" (80). As it applies to the orphans, the refrain suggests each child's potential for greatness, for having happy lives despite their beginnings. According to Homer, the refrain is actually a "benediction" and "full of hope" to remind the orphans that "they *were* the heroes of their own lives" (80). In the novel's larger construct, the refrain also complements other characters' lives. Ray Kendall is metaphorically a hero in that he raises Candy once her mother dies, and he is a self-taught, skilled mechanic whose skills and hands are often equated with those of a surgeon. Wally Worthington—his last name is symbolic—has princely and kingly qualities. Dr. Larch even says that Wally has the "body of a hero . . . and the face of a benefactor," and Homer thinks, "I have met a Prince of Maine. . . . I have seen a King of New England" (197). Both Larch and Homer typify noble qualities. Larch's noble qualities are evident when he opens the orphanage and when he either delivers mothers or babies. Homer's princely qualities are evident throughout the narration in his devotion to those around him—Angel, Candy, Wally, Olive Worthington, and Ray Kendall. When Larch dies, Homer returns to St. Cloud's to carry on Larch's mission, or, symbolically, the prince robes himself in the dead king's mantle. As the concluding sentence affirms, "there was no fault to be found in the hearts of either Dr. Stone or Dr. Larch, who were—if there ever were—Princes of Maine, Kings of New England" (552).

As do the other novels, *Cider House* ends affirmatively. To atone for violating a moral rule and to keep Rose Rose from being arrested, Mr. Rose quietly bleeds to death while she escapes, and he wants his death recorded as a suicide. Melony not only reconciles with Lorna but also with life's rules and is finally relaxed, contented, and happy. She wills her body to St. Cloud's, but Homer knows she has returned home, buries her under the apple trees on the hill, and acknowledges that Melony "had truly educated him, she had shown him the light. She was more Sunshine than he ever was. . . . 'Let us be happy for Melony,' he said to himself. 'Melony has found a family' " (551). The most life-confirming actions involve Homer and Candy, who end their affair because, to quote Homer, "We're doing the wrong thing. . . . It's time to do everything right" (473); accordingly, they tell Wally and Angel the "whole story." Wally and Candy "throw themselves full tilt into apple farming. Wally would serve two terms as president of the Maine Horticultural Society; Candy would serve a term as director of the New York-New England Apple Institute" (549). Even the caliber of migrant workers improves—Jamaicans who "were friendly, nonviolent, and good workers. . . . They knew how to handle fruit and they never hurt each other" (544). Angel would spend equal time with Homer and with Candy and Wally and would become a fiction writer. Larch's scheme succeeds, and Homer returns to St. Cloud's, becomes Dr. Stone, and carries on Larch's crusade. The novel ends where it began—at St. Cloud's, but now the landscape's darkness has been softened with images of light and promise, "There was no fault to be found in the hearts of either Dr. Stone or Dr. Larch who were . . . Princes of Maine, Kings of New England" (552).

Cider House also indicated some major technical and stylistic changes for Irving. For example, bears, Vienna, sport metaphors, narratives within the main narrative, and lurking symbols of evil like the Under Toad and Sorrow, are noticeably absent. In addition, Irving returns to the third-person omniscient narrator that worked so well in *Garp* and that serves a similar function in *Cider House*—to chronicle a number of lives from youth to maturity. The plot is just as entertaining and suspenseful as those in the other novels, but as Irving emphasizes: "I believe I'm in much better control of the narrative pace now. I can make it slow down like molasses or make 15 years disappear without using four chapters. . . . I couldn't have done that 10 years ago."[9] Irving is probably referring to the novel's tenth chapter entitled "Fifteen Years," which spans fifteen years in the major and minor characters' lives.

Irving's expansive plots, meaningful chapter titles, and epilogues evoke the Victorian novels, particularly those of Charles Dickens, whose *David Copperfield* and *Great Expectations* comprise the nightly readings in the boys' dormitory in *Cider House*. In addition, Irving's style in *Cider House* indicates Dickensian touches, especially in establishing characters through certain idiosyncracies. Mrs. Grogan, for example, is linked with her Cardinal Newman prayer, and the robust Winkles—a name Dickens would have appreciated—are associated with their love of the outdoors, particularly in the river scene as they bounce up and down in the rushing waters "like giant, blond otters" (44). His runny nose and "I'm having a bad day" characterize Curly Day. A speech impediment characterizes young David Copperfield, who calls Homer "Gomer" and Nurse Edna "Medna." This behavior infuriates Curly, who corrects Copperfield with, "It's *Homer*, you idiot. . . . It's *Edna*, you little scum" (170, 171). Even Curly's bullying the younger, smaller Copperfield has a Dickensian flair. These Dickensian touches enhance both the characterizations and the narrative.

The William Morrow Company would publish *Cider House* and *Owen Meany*. According to Irving, after Henry Robbins died, Jane Rosenman, a young Dutton editor, "did a good job" editing *Hotel New Hampshire*, but adds Irving: "And then I met Harvey Ginsberg, who was actually an old friend of Henry's—a classmate at Harvard—and just when I'm writing *The Cider House Rules*, where does it turn out that Harvey is from? Bangor, Maine. . . . And so now Harvey and I are together at William Morrow, and I'm so happy I don't have plans to change publishing houses. How many writers do you know who'll say that? Hear many happy publishing stories?"[10]

Cider House sold well, was on the *New York Times* best-seller list, and was the Book-of-the-Month Club's 1985 summer selection. As with Irving's other novels, reviewers and critics praised and damned *Cider House*. At one extreme were the praises of Benjamin DeMott and Christopher Lehmann-Haupt, who both ranked *Cider House* above *Garp* and *Hotel New Hampshire*. DeMott thought that the "storytelling" was "straightforward" and the theme in "firm focus,"[11] an idea Lehmann-Haupt underscored in his comment that the plot of *Cider House* was "more controlled and pointed."[12] In contrast, Walter Clemons and Anthony Burgess lambasted both the novel's plot and characterizations.[13] The most scathing comment came from Roger Lewis who called *Cider House* a "thick brick of a book" that deserved "to be thrown back through John Irving's window. A black comedy about abortion is not funny, not because abortion can't be made funny but because Irving isn't a comedian."[14] Between these two extremes, however, were Carol C. Harter and James R. Thompson, who admired *Cider House* for its "vigorous personal vision," its "richly textured" characterizations, and its "purely human drama," but who noted the novel's "minor lapses"—the "labored prose or caseworker talk, little litanies repeated with maddening frequencies . . . kisses in embarrassing abundance, and pages drenched in superfluous tears."[15]

Cider House may or may not rank above *Garp* or *Hotel New Hampshire*, and it may or may not be a "thick brick of a book." Yet, in its settings, characters, situations, and themes, *Cider House* marks a definite maturing in Irving's literary talents, which would be honed even finer in *A Prayer for Owen Meany*.

NOTES

1. Delores A. Barclay, "Writing Across a Landscape," *Memphis Commercial Appeal*, July 21, 1985, J5.
2. John Irving, *The Cider House Rules*, 19; hereafter cited in the text.
3. Esther B. Fein, "Costly Pleasures," *New York Times Book Review*, May 26, 1985, 25.
4. *Ibid.*
5. Carol C. Harter and James R. Thompson, *John Irving*, 127.
6. Fein, "Costly Pleasures," 25.
7. *Ibid.*
8. Benjamin DeMott, "Guilt and Compassion," *New York Times Book Review*, May 26, 1985, 1.
9. Barclay, "Writing Across a Landscape," J5.
10. Ron Hansen, "The Art of Fiction XCIII: John Irving," *Paris Review*, 28. 100 (1986): 103.
11. DeMott, "Guilt and Compassion," 1.
12. Christopher Lehmann-Haupt, *New York Times*, 20 May 1985, C20.
13. Walter Clemons, "Dr. Larch's Odd Orphanage," *Newsweek* 105 (27 May 1985): 80. Anthony Burgess, "A Novel of Obstetrics," *Atlantic Monthly*, 256. 1 (July 1985): 99–100.
14. Roger Lewis, "Larger Than Life," *New Statesman*, 109 (28 June 1985): 29.
15. Harter and Thompson, *John Irving*, 142.

CHAPTER EIGHT

"The Magnitude of a Miracle": *A Prayer for Owen Meany* (1989)

Irving's *A Prayer for Owen Meany* contains no bears, no Vienna, no World War II, and no rapes. However, it does contain a boy's school, Gravesend Academy; a sports metaphor, slam-dunking basketballs; a war, the Vietnam War; dual settings in the United States and Canada; and violence. The major difference, however, between this novel and Irving's preceding ones is that it is ultimately about religious faith and miracles, a theme absent in the other novels. In commenting about *Owen Meany*, Irving emphasizes, "I've always asked myself what would be the magnitude of the miracle that could convince me of religious faith."[1] This idea is the novel's core and controls the settings, characters, themes, and literary techniques.

Like *Cider House*, the setting is not expansive, and except for sporadic scene shifts to Sawyer's Depot in northern New Hampshire, the University of New Hampshire at Durham, and Phoenix and Fort Huachuca in Arizona, the primary setting is Gravesend, New Hampshire, where protagonists John Wheelwright and Owen Meany experience their rites of passage. Gravesend's history is linked with the novel's religious theme since Reverend John

Wheelwright, the protagonist's ancestor, founded the town when he was banished from the Massachusetts Bay Colony because he proposed radical religious beliefs. Indeed, John claims that "his own religious confusion, and stubbornness, owe much to my ancestor."[2] In Gravesend is the Wheelwrights' "grand, brick, Federal monster of a house" (26), the scene for major portions of the novel's actions. While the home suggests permanency amid change, John will eventually forsake home and country when he emigrates to Canada after Owen Meany's tragic death. Dan Needham, John's stepfather, often asks him to return, but John says, "Although I enjoy my visits, not even the tempting nostalgia of the house at 80 Front Street could entice me to return to the United States" (461). John thus becomes Irving's only protagonist who abandons his ancestral home for a self-imposed isolation in a foreign country. In this sense, too, Gravesend is important because it represents small-town life that is forever changed because of the Vietnam War.

Whereas in the other novels a foreign place, usually Vienna, suggests the *Anschluss*-spawned violence, in *Owen Meany* Canada represents a relatively calm refuge that contrasts with the violent anti-Vietnam War demonstrations and protests that are racking the United States. John Wheelwright even says that the Canadians calmly welcomed the American draft dodgers and war resisters. For example, even though he often apologizes, "I'm not really a draft dodger," he quickly realizes that "most Canadians didn't care *what* I was [and] didn't care *why* I'd come; they didn't ask any questions. It was 1968, probably the midpoint of Vietnam 'resisters' coming to Canada; most Canadians were sympathetic—they thought the war in Vietnam was stupid and wrong, too" (401). Canada's relatively calm attitude is also evident when John notes that even the most militant American resisters in Canada, the Union of American Exiles, are a "pretty tame lot" when "compared to Hester—and her SDS friends" (402).

Partly to protest the Vietnam War but mainly in anger because of Owen's death, John crosses the New Hampshire-Canadian border in 1968, the year Owen is killed. Although his defection to Canada is supposed to be a "very forceful political statement," John admits that he "never had to suffer" because with his teaching experience at Gravesend Academy, his graduate degree, and his sound recommendations, he becomes "instantly respectable and almost immediately employed" (402, 403). John's expatriate life in Canada also heightens his alienation and isolation, especially since he teaches at Bishop Strachan School for Girls, where he is often the only male teacher.

Regarding John's self-imposed isolation and alienation in Canada, Dan Needham, his foster father, counsels: "Let bygones be bygones—not even Owen would *still* be angry. Do you think Owen Meany would have blamed the whole country for what happened to him? That was madness; this is madness, too" (462). Canada thus becomes the setting in which John assuages his anger by rekindling his faith. He says that he is different from most Americans who fled to Canada because he has "the church; don't underestimate the church—its healing power, and the comforting way it can set you apart. . . . And so the first Canadians I knew were churchgoers—an almost universally helpful lot, and much less confused and troubled than the few Americans I'd met in Toronto (and *most* Americans I had known at home)" (403). Although he wrestles with his faith for the twenty years he lives in

Canada, John's "*oral* history" (27) concludes with his renewed faith as he prays for himself and for Owen Meany. Metaphorically, just as Vienna teaches Irving's other characters about the world's ways, Canada teaches John about the ways of faith.

Irving says that in *Owen Meany* he wanted "to create two victims of the Vietnam period in our history,"[3] and one is John Wheelwright, the narrator-protagonist. Unlike Irving's other protagonists, John is mainly an observer and reporter instead of a principal actor in the plot, and various plot details emphasize his neutral role. During the Christmas pageant at Christ Church, for example, John plays Saint Joseph, a role requiring neither words nor actions. Even when he and Owen practice the slam-dunk shot, John says that "my part in this exercise was extremely limited" (475). In addition, John never has a girl friend, is never sexually initiated, and he sadly admits, "I was twenty-one and I was still a Joseph; I was a Joseph then, and I'm just a Joseph now" (389). When Owen cuts off John's right index finger to keep him out of the draft, John becomes even more isolated and alienated from his own generation. During a Vietnam War demonstration in Washington, for instance, John carries no placard and admits:

> But I tried to feel I was part of the demonstration; sadly, I *didn't* feel I was part of it—I didn't feel I was part of anything. I had a 4-F deferment; I would never have to go to war, or to Canada. By the simple act of removing the first two joints of my right index finger, Owen Meany had enabled me to feel completely detached from my generation. (470)

His further detachment and alienation also result when he moves to Canada but still craves news about the United States. As Canon Mackie gently reminds him, "You're a Canadian citizen, but what are you always talking about? You talk about America more than any American I know" (204).

Indirectly, John becomes a Vietnam War victim. In 1968, the year Owen will die, John has completed his master's degree, will enter the Ph.D. program at the University of Massachusetts in the fall, and his student deferment plus his missing index finger will keep him out of the service. Moreover, because his grandmother finances his education, John confesses: "If I was thinking anything—if I was thinking at all—I was considering that my life had become a kind of doorstep-sitting, watching the parades pass by . . . I wasn't doing anything; there wasn't anything I had to do" (507). Finally, Owen Meany's death affects John the most. He says that both he and Hester were "damaged by what happened to Owen," and adds, "What has happened to me has simply *neutered* me. I just don't feel like 'practicing' " (453).

Besides being an integral part of the novel's bildungsroman motif, John Wheelwright is necessary for the novel's religious theme. The narrative is not only John's prayer for Owen Meany, but the plot also analyzes various aspects of faith in the contemporary world. Whereas in *Cider House* Larch and Homer believed in private religious views and prayers, in *Owen Meany* the dramatic opening sentence announces the theme, "I am doomed to remember a boy with a wrecked voice—not because of his voice, or because he was the smallest person I ever knew, or even because he was the instrument of my mother's death, but because he is the reason I believe in God; I am a Christian because of Owen Meany'' (13).

Recounted twenty years after his emigration to Canada and Owen's death, John Wheelwright's narration traces the development of his own confused faith. He was baptized as a Congregationalist, confirmed as an Episcopalian, and finally becomes an Anglican with a ''church-rummage faith—the kind that needs patching up every weekend'' (14). Significantly, too, as in most hagiographies, John's faith has often been tested by adversities that include his mother's death, the Vietnam War, and especially Owen Meany's tragic death. However, not only is the last chapter, ''The Shot,'' a typical Irving epilogue that details the characters' fates but also the chapter's last five sections become both John's catharsis and the novel's main thrust. After *almost* concluding his story, John adds:

> Let's see: there's not much else—there's almost nothing to add. Only this: that it took years for me to face my memory of how Owen Meany died—and once I forced myself to remember the details, I could never forget how he died; I will never forget it. I am doomed to remember this. (506)

How Owen died explains all that preceded it—the novel's armless symbols, Owen's prophecies and life's mission, and the reason for practicing ''the shot.'' Besides becoming the novel's affirmative vision, the chapter's closing paragraphs are John's prayer for Owen Meany as well as John's testimony about his own faith that has been rekindled and strengthened because Owen ''had been a hero'' and a ''miracle too'' (542). After admitting that he is ''always saying prayers'' for Owen, John confirms that Owen symbolized those ''forces we didn't have the faith to feel,

they were the forces we failed to believe in—and they were also lifting Owen Meany, taking him out of our hands. O God—please give him back! I shall keep asking You'' (542–43). John's quiet, reverent prayer not only assuages the novel's general chaos and confusion, but it explains his opening comments that what faith he has in God he owes to Owen Meany.

In contrast with John's observer-reporter role, Owen Meany is the novel's central focus because he is the principal actor. He hits the foul ball that kills John's mother, and this act convinces Owen that he is God's instrument. He also suggests and directs the games that he, John, Hester, Noah, and Simon play. Owen also directs the Christmas pageant at Christ Church when he suggests dynamic changes in staging and the actors' roles; similarly, he is instrumental in changing Dan Needham's ideas about staging and roles in *A Christmas Carol*. At Gravesend Academy where he edits *The Grave*, the campus newspaper, he is nicknamed ''the Voice'' for his outspoken editorials that criticize school policies and headmasters, especially the ingratiating Randy White. In addition, Owen is directly responsible for the fiascoes involving Dr. Dolder's Volkswagen and Mary Magdalene's statue, both of which appear on the Main Academy Building's stage. Finally, Owen subtly severs his relationship with Hester, decides that he must cut John's finger off to save him from the war, and he always insists that he and John practice ''the shot.''

Owen becomes, furthermore, a victim of the Vietnam War, and Irving tells Phyllis Robinson that he ''wanted to create two markedly dissimilar victims of the war, one a hero, the other a defector.''[4] That Owen will be a hero is evident, first of all, in his desire to serve in Vietnam. As he tells John, "IT'S NOT THAT I *WANT* TO GO TO VIETNAM—IT'S WHERE I HAVE TO GO. IT'S WHERE I'M A HERO. I'VE GOT TO BE THERE" (417). When John thinks Owen is joking, Owen ominously emphasizes:

> I'M NOT PLAYING AROUND. . . . WOULD I REQUEST A COMBAT ASSIGNMENT IF I WERE PLAYING AROUND? . . . I SAVE LOTS OF CHILDREN. . . . THAT'S HOW I KNOW WHERE I AM—THEY'RE DEFINITELY VIETNAMESE CHILDREN, AND I SAVE THEM. (418)

Owen's prophecies come true when, in an ironic plot twist, Owen saves John and the Vietnamese children, not in Vietnam, but rather in a temporary rest room at the Phoenix airport.

In terms of the novel's religious theme, Irving says, "Jesus has always struck me as the perfect victim and perfect hero,"[5] and loose parallels exist between Christ and Owen Meany. When Owen first meets the Eastman children while they play in the Wheelwrights' attic, John emphasizes Owen's divine appearance, halo and all:

> The powerful morning sun struck Owen's head from above, and from a little behind him, so that the light itself seemed to be presenting him . . . there is no doubt that, in the dazzling configurations of the sun that poured through the attic skylight, he looked like a descending angel—a tiny but fiery god, sent to adjudicate the errors of our ways (71).

More specifically, Owen plays the Christ child in the Christmas pageant, and in *A Christmas Carol*, he is the Ghost of Christmas Future and, instead of Scrooge's name and dates on the tombstone, Owen sees his name and the date of his own death. As "the Voice" of Gravesend Academy, Owen makes enemies with his tirades against hypocrisy, injustice, and Philistinism. Old Thorny, the retired, benign headmaster, warns Owen: "You've made more enemies in less than two years than I've made in twenty! Be careful you don't give your enemies a way to get you" (271). When his enemies find a way "to get" him, John emphasizes a Christlike fate, "the Executive Committee crucified Owen Meany—they axed him; they gave him the boot; they threw him out" (354).

In addition to Owen's unique voice—John says Owen's voice is "not entirely of this world" (16)—Owen writes and speaks in capital letters, an idea Irving adopted from "editions of the New Testament in which Jesus' utterances appear in red letters."[6] Owen, of course, occasionally quotes biblical passages: "FATHER, FORGIVE THEM; FOR THEY KNOW NOT WHAT THEY DO" (339); "WOE UNTO THEM THAT CALL EVIL GOOD AND GOOD EVIL" (351); "WHOSOEVER LIVETH AND BELIEVETH IN ME SHALL NEVER DIE" (541). Another loose parallel is that Owen's life and actions strengthen Dan Needham's faith and restore John's and Reverend Lewis Merrill's faiths. Not only does Owen selflessly sacrifice his own life for John and the Vietnamese refugees, but Owen's preknowledge about his own death is similar to Christ's knowledge. As Phyllis Robinson notes: "The part of Jesus himself that most impresses Irving, 'the biggest miracle of them all,' is that Christ knows what is going to happen to him. 'That is truly a heroic burden to carry.' "[7]

Like Susie in *Hotel New Hampshire* and Melony in *Cider House*, Hester Eastman is big-boned and big-bosomed—"her body belonged in the jungle" (263)—but unlike these other heroines, she is very attractive and sings beautifully. Because she is older than John or Owen, she is more worldly wise, especially in sexual matters, earning her the nickname ''Hester the Molester.'' Although John is attracted to Hester, she is attracted to Owen and sexually initiates him, and they eventually fall in love. Because she believes that women should have equal rights, her alienation from her family inexorably begins when the Eastmans plan to send Noah and Simon to Gravesend Academy but make no plans for Hester's future: ''Hester was in as much need of rescuing from the wildness within *her*—and from the rural north country rituals of her sex—as Noah and Simon were in need of saving'' (239). As Owen foretells, ''THAT'S WHEN HESTER WENT ON THE WARPATH'' (239). Hester's warpaths include various affairs—all designed ''to educate her parents regarding the error of their ways'' (249). Hester's wild rebelliousness will also spur her to join the decade's demonstrations protesting the Vietnam War.

If *Owen Meany* ''grew out of Irving's conviction that the Vietnam War made victims of us all, not just those who were killed or who left their country,''[8] then Hester is just as much a victim as are John and Owen. Although Hester and Owen love each other, the Vietnam War thwarts their potential for forming a solid family basis when he decides to become an Army officer, and she becomes a war protester. In addition, even though she wants to marry Owen, he refuses because he has foreseen his fate. His refusal actually proves just how much he loves her, and John says, ''I think I know what he was doing; he was helping her to fall out of love with him before he died'' (476). Even so, Owen's death affects her: ''Hester was damaged by what happened to Owen Meany; I'm sure she thinks she was damaged even more than I was damaged. . . . We were both damaged by what happened to Owen'' (453–54). After Owen's death, Hester never becomes ''seriously involved'' again because he had been the ''love of her life'' (453).

When she becomes a hard-rock singer—she adopts her childhood nickname Hester the Molester—her voice is ''equivalent to an abused woman crying for help from the bottom of an iron barrel'' (453). Her ''truly ugly'' videos depict:

> carnal encounters with unidentified young boys intercut with black-and-white, documentary footage from the Vietnam War. Napalm victims, mothers cradling their murdered children, helicopters landing and taking off and crashing in the midst of perilous ground fire, emergency surgeries in the field, countless GI's with their heads in their hands—and Hester herself entering and leaving different but similar hotel rooms, wherein a sheepish young boy is always putting on or just taking off his clothes. (453)

Even her song titles reflect her life's circumstances, especially as they refer to Owen's life and death: ''Gone to Arizona'' (where Owen is stationed); ''You Won't See Me at His Funeral'' (Hester's words to Owen); ''Drivin' with No Hands'' (Owen's arms are blown off below the elbows); ''There's No Forgettin' Nineteen Sixty-eight'' (the year Owen died); ''Just Another Dead Hero'' (the futility of Owen's and other Americans' deaths during the Vietnam War). As John also points out, the irony is that ''out of Owen's suffering, and her own, Hester has made a mindless muddle of sex and protest, which young girls who have *never* suffered feel they can 'relate to' '' (454). Significantly, however, as do Irving's other strong heroines, Hester confronts life's forces and survives: ''I admire her—she's certainly been a more heroic survivor that I've been, and her kind of survival is admirable'' (504).

Tabitha Wheelwright, John's mother, typifies Irving's strong motherly figures. When she becomes pregnant, for example, she easily transcends her ''little fling,'' gets ''over Lewis Merrill rather quickly,'' and bears ''up better than stoically to the task of bearing his illegitimate child'' (482). She is also a loving person who, to quote John, wants ''nothing from life but a child and a loving husband; it is important to note these *singulars*—she did not want children, she wanted . . . *just* me and she got me; she did not want men in her life, she wanted a man, the *right* man, and shortly before she died, she found him'' (44). Not only does she become a ''perfect mother'' for John, but she becomes a surrogate mother for Owen Meany and thus emphasizes the less-than-motherly image cast by Mrs. Meany. Tabitha loves Owen as if he were her son, often drives him home, promises that she will see that he is admitted to Gravesend Academy, and will even buy him the proper school clothes. Her death is significant for the novel's religious theme because Owen believes that he has become God's instrument through the foul ball that struck Tabitha down. In addition, when John recalls his mother's death, he realizes: ''That was when I first began to think about certain events or specific things being 'important' and having 'special purposes' . . . I was not what was commonly called a believer then, and I am a believer now: I believe in God, and I believe in the 'special purpose' of certain events or special things'' (83). Finally, not only do memories of her have a healing effect on those whom she cherished and loved, but the dressmaker's dummy clad in her red dress soothes Lewis Merrill's tormented conscience and then restores his dead faith.

In referring to his stepfather, John says, "Dan Needham is the best father a boy could have" (372). Although Dan is a loving, caring stepfather, he does not become overly protective as were Bogus Trumper, Severin Winter, or Garp. Instead, Dan Needham is more of John's best  friend and counsellor. For example, while his mother's other suitors are all handsome and bring ridiculous gifts ranging from "rubber ducks for the bath" to Fowler's *Modern English Usage*, Dan is "tall and gawky" and brings John a stuffed armadillo—"the first present any of my mother's 'beaus' gave me that I kept" (50, 53). John then adds, "But he knew very well what a six-year-old was like; to his credit, Dan Needham was always a little bit of a six-year-old himself" (53). When John's mother is killed, Dan also helps John understand why Owen gives him the baseball card collection: "to show me how sorry he was about the accident, and how much he was hurting, too—because Owen had loved my mother almost as much as I did" (81–82).

Within the plot, Dan Needham proposes a positive alternative despite life's inexplicable forces. When Owen returns the armadillo *sans* claws, Dan explains that the clawless animal represents all of them—"We've lost part of ourselves"—but he then concludes: "There was no way any of this *was* acceptable! What had happened was unacceptable. Yet we still had to live with it" (85). Dan's positive approach to the injustice of Tabitha's death is to devote himself to teaching, "Like many dedicated educators, Dan Needham had made education his religion" (238). He becomes a "good, spirited" teacher who believes it is "more difficult to be a teenager than a grown-up" but who also is more compassionate toward the elderly who are "suffering a second adolescence and . . . required special care" (237). Dan's admirable fatherly virtues and his positive approach to life and faith contrast with Reverend Lewis Merrill, John Wheelwright's natural father.

While necessary for the novel's suspense regarding the identity of John's real father, Reverend Lewis Merrill is more significant for the novel's religious theme. While John's mother stoically transcends their affair, Merrill wallows in self-guilt and pity. However, when he sees her at the baseball game and realizes that he is still attracted to her, Merrill is ashamed and wishes that she would "drop dead" (481). At that moment, Owen hits the fatal foul ball, and Merrill believes that "God had punished him; God had taught Pastor Merrill not to trifle with prayer" (481). Merrill believes that he is now outside God's mercy and grace, and his faith dies. As John reminds him: "You're always talking about 'doubt as the essence and not the opposite of faith'—but it seems to me that *your* doubt has taken control of you. I think that's what Owen thought about you, too" (478). Merrill's stutter symbolizes his lack of religious conviction and courage, and his stutter is especially evident as he talks to John about faith and miracles: "You want to call Owen, and everything that happened to him, a m-m-*miracle*. . . . You sound positively *converted*. . . . I would be careful not to confuse your g-g-g-grief with genuine, religious belief" (478).

Even as they talk, Merrill does not understand the miracle that occurs when he speaks "in the exact falsetto, the 'permanent scream' " of Owen's voice, which reveals the exact location of the fatal foul ball (479). However, John recognizes the miracle, "That was the first time that Owen Meany let me hear from him—after he was gone . . . Owen promised me that God would tell me who my father was'' (479). After learning from Dan that Merrill had ''once tried to be brave and honorable'' regarding his affair with John's mother, John decides that he could teach Merrill ''how to pray again'' and ''have a little faith'' (487). John takes his mother's dressmaker's dummy, places it under the chancel windows, and throws the fated baseball through one of the stained-glass windows. Merrill rushes out, sees the dummy, imagines it is John's mother, and says: ''God—forgive me! Tabby—I didn't tell him! I promised you I wouldn't and I didn't . . . Tabby—forgive me, please!'' (490). He falls on his side, draws his knees up, and babbles incoherently. Symbolically, Merrill's confession and repentance become his catharsis, and his faith is restored as evident when he begins the prayers at Owen Meany's funeral:

> '' 'I am the resurrection and the life, saith the Lord . . . ' '' my father began. There was something newly powerful and confident in his voice, and the mourners heard it; the congregation gave him their complete attention. Of course, I knew what it was that had changed him; he had found his lost faith—he spoke with absolute belief in every word he uttered; therefore, he never stuttered. (497)

In *Owen Meany*, violence does not stalk the main characters' lives as relentlessly as it does in the other novels. There are, however, bizarre deaths. The foul ball kills John's mother, and Owen Meany's mother burns to death when the American flag she drapes herself in catches fire as she sits too close to the fireplace. Grandmother Wheelwright dies in her sleep at the Gravesend Retreat for the Elderly with a television remote-control switch in her hand in ''such a way that the channels kept changing . . .

looking for something good'' (466). If the *Anschluss* spawns World War II's violence in the earlier novels, then the Vietnam War spawns some of the violence and death in *Owen Meany*. Indeed, the references to the number of Americans continually sent to die in the war underscore the escalation of the U.S. intervention in Vietnam.

In addition to the deaths of Owen, the Jarvits, and even Mrs. Meany, other specific deaths result either directly or indirectly from the war. For example, as he was urinating under a tree outside of a Vietnam whorehouse, Harry Hoyt dies when he is bitten by a Russell's viper (121). In an attempt to evade the draft, Buzzy Thurston drinks a ''fifth of bourbon a day for two weeks'' (122), smokes large quantities of marijuana, takes LSD, and even eats his Hawaiian shirt ''including the buttons and the contents of the pocket'' (122). Although he is ''declared psychologically unfit,'' Buzzy becomes so addicted to these drugs that he crashes his car into a bridge abutment on Maiden Hill Road a short distance from the Meany Granite Quarry. Mrs. Hoyt, who is forced out of Gravesend because she is a war resister, believes that Buzzy is ''simply another victim of the Vietnam War; although no one listened to her, she maintained that the war was the cause of many abuses Buzzy had practiced upon himself—just as surely as the war had axed her Harry'' (123).

Another Vietnam War victim is Warrant Officer Frank Jarvits who, during his third tour in Vietnam, is burned to death while refueling a helicopter in what Major Rawls calls ''some stupid asshole mistake'' (524). Rawls likewise underscores the war's psychological effects on Frank who spent his furloughs ''looking in his neighbors' windows through a telescopic sight . . . lining up everyone in the cross hairs! If he hadn't gone back to 'Nam, he'd have gone to jail'' (519). Indirectly, Dick Jarvits, Frank's brother, is a Vietnam War victim. He dresses in jungle fatigues complete with crossed-cartridge belts, and he carries an entrenching tool, a bayonet, and a machete. His room at home reeks of marijuana, is filled with Vietnam souvenirs, and where, says John, Dick probably dreams ''without cease of butchering the Viet Cong'' (527). According to Rawls, while Frank may have been ''wackier,'' Dick is the ''chief wacko—he hangs around the airport all day, watching the planes, talking to soldiers. He can't wait to be old enough to go to 'Nam'' (519). When he sees the Vietnamese children, Dick goes berserk, throws a Chicom grenade into the airport rest room, mortally wounds Owen, and is killed by Major Rawls who breaks Dick's neck with the dull edge of Dick's machete.

Of all the family images in Irving's novels, the Jarvits provide the most negative image. They live in a low-income housing development ''distinguished by a large population of dismantled automobiles—indeed there were more cars on cinder blocks, with their wheels off or their engines ripped out from under their hoods, than there were *live* cars parked at the curb or in driveways'' (524). The mother is a foul-mouthed termagant. According to her daughter, the mother will spit in Owen's face as he presents her with the American flag at the funeral. The father is a bullying drunkard and is not Frank's or Dick's natural father. As Rawls explains, ''This clown's the father of that unfortunate girl—I can't tell you who knocked her up, but I've got the feeling it was a family affair. My odds are on the warrant officer. . . . Maybe *both* brothers were banging her'' (519–20). Although the daughter is polite to Owen and John, she hates Frank, her half-brother: ''If Vietnam hadn't killed that bastard, somethin' else would have—that's what *I* say'' (526). As evidenced by their neighborhood and life, the Jarvits, along with their relatives from Yuma and Modesto, are a transient family without solid roots, and they never form a solid family unit as a protection against life's forces. As John notes, the Jarvits are a ''family torn in halves, or worse'' (519).

The other family images contrast with the Jarvits. Before and after his mother is killed, John not only emphasizes the solid family bonds between him, his mother, and Dan Needham, but also between his grandmother and her house servants, Lydia and Germaine. Though eccentric, the Meanys are a family unit, and Mr. Meany dutifully chauffeurs Owen around and loves him. However, some of these family units disintegrate. Although John often returns for visits, he abandons his ancestral home, emigrates to Canada, and never marries, and so the Wheelwright name will die out. Mr. Meany lives a lonely life as a meter reader for the electric company after his wife burns to death. Whether Irving intends these disintegrations as symbols of the Vietnam War's effects is tenuous, but the fact remains that Owen's death causes John's emigration and the further decline of the Meany family. Along with the Wheelwrights' name, the Meany and Jarvits family names will die out, thus symbolizing the Vietnam War's far-reaching effects.

On the other hand, the Eastman family epitomizes an Irvingesque family solidarity. They adapt to the world's changing ways—they easily change from selling lumber to real estate: ''In New Hampshire, that's what you have left to sell after you've cut down the trees'' (22). John underscores the Eastmans' virtues: ''But in the summer of

'62, I thought my Aunt Martha and Uncle Alfred were a *perfect* couple; and yet they depressed me because of how happy they were. In their happiness they reminded me of the brief time my mother and Dan Needham had been together—and how happy they'd been too'' (373). Even the Eastmans' later years are happy and fulfilling. Noah and Simon marry, have families, and ''do an admirable job of looking after Old Uncle Alfred and my Aunt Martha, who is still a lovely woman. . . . The Eastman Company had provided him and my Aunt Martha with a good and long life'' (372). Although Hester may be their ''only unhappiness,'' the family optimistically believes that she will return home one Christmas—''that's what she says'' (372).

In the winter, Owen enjoys basketball—''God knows why!'' says John—and Owen becomes especially obsessed with ''an impossible frill of the game ('impossible' for him): the slam-dunk'' (271), a ritual Owen and John practice religiously. In practicing ''the shot,'' as they call it, Owen dribbles toward the basket, times his jump, leaps into John's arms, and is then boosted above the basket's rim. They perfect their technique and reduce the time from ten to three seconds. Their slam-dunks become the novel's sports metaphor. As do wrestling in *Garp* and weight lifting in *Hotel New Hampshire*, slam-dunking prepares them for struggling against life's traumas, an idea John underscores when he says that it is ''such a ridiculous thing for him to want to do—for someone his size to set himself the challenge of soaring and reaching so high'' (271–72). Moreover, when the Gravesend Academy basketball coach jokes that he may even use him in a game, Owen replies, ''IT'S NOT FOR A GAME'' (272). In a typical Irvingesque plot twist, the reason for practicing "the shot" in under four seconds becomes evident when Dick Jarvits throws the grenade into the men's room, and John lifts Owen to the window ledge where he cradles the grenade as it detonates and blows off Owen's arms at the elbows. Furthermore, "the shot" highlights the religious theme, especially in the scene in which Owen wants the time clock set to three seconds and says: "IF WE CAN DO IT UNDER FOUR SECONDS, WE CAN DO IT UNDER THREE . . . IT JUST TAKES A LITTLE MORE FAITH . . . FAITH TAKES PRACTICE" (304).

In addition to the foul ball that represents life's ubiquitous forces, the other symbols in *Owen Meany* are the three armless figures: Watahantowet, the armadillo, and Mary Magdalene's statue. Watahantowet is the Indian sagamore who sells John's ancestor the land on which Gravesend is founded. Watahantowet signs the deed with his mark, a totem of an armless man. Various theories explain the totem's significance: that it represents Watahantowet's feelings about selling the land—it is equivalent to having "his arms cut off"; that though armless, Watahantowet holds a feather in his mouth to symbolize "his frustration about not being able to write"; that he holds a tomahawk in his mouth to symbolize "no arms . . . Watahantowet does not fight" (19). Each interpretation relates to Owen Meany's ultimate fate since he loses his arms when the grenade detonates. In other words, Owen has given his arms and life for his country; he has kept a diary but will never be able to write again if he lives; and he "does not fight" in Vietnam.

The clawless armadillo represents Owen's remorse for having accidentally killed John's mother. As Dan Needham explains, "Don't you see, Johnny? If he could, he would cut off his *hands* for you—that's how it makes him feel, to have *touched* that baseball bat'' (85). Later, of course, in the airport rest room, Owen literally loses his hands for John and the refugees. In pranking the Gravesend Academy's Executive Committee, and in particular Randy White, Owen cuts Mary Magdalene's statue from its base and before bolting it to the stage floor, he cuts off the statue's head and the arms just below the elbows ''so that her gesture of beseeching the assembled audience would seem all the more an act of supplication—all the more helpless'' (357). Symbolically, Owen is indeed helpless when the Executive Committee expels him, and he is even more helpless as he is dying and attempts to reach out to John—''I think he wanted to touch me. That was when he realized that his arms were gone'' (541).

Owen Meany was on the *New York Times* best-seller list, was the Book-of-the-Month Club's main selection for March 1989, and received mixed critical receptions. In praising *Owen Meany*, R. Z. Sheppard writes that John Wheelwright's ''challenge to faith'' (when the foul ball kills his mother) is ''vintage Irving'' because the accident is ''simultaneously horrifying and absurdly funny''; that the novel is a ''fable of political predestination''; and that the novel will interest ''symbol hunters'' from sophomores who argue about the symbolical significance of the declawed armadillo to graduate students who note that Owen Meany ''shares more than initials with Oskar Matzerath, the runt hero of Günter Grass's *The Tin Drum*.''[9] Sheppard then concludes: ''As usual, Irving delivers a boisterous cast, a spirited story line and a quality of prose that is frequently underestimated, even by his admirers. . . . Irving's litany of error and folly may strike some as too righteous; but it is effective.''[10] According to William Pritchard, ''*The Cider House Rules* was a recovery from the silliness of much of *The Hotel New Hampshire*, partly because it was a book about abortion that truly explored the issue [and] Irving managed to restrain his usual proclivity for . . . the 'cute and trendy,' but 'cute' is precisely the word that *A Prayer for Owen Meany* invites.''[11] Pritchard also says that John Wheelwright is a ''lackluster character of little interest,'' but Pritchard did admire the novel's ''superbly narrated sequences of comic action,'' especially the scene about the descent of Dr. Dolder's Volkswagen down the marble steps of Gravesend's Main Academy Building.[12]

Barbara Hoffert thinks that the reader will be interested in the developing friendship between John Wheelwright and Owen Meany as well as in the novel's mysteries—why Wheelwright is a Christian and who his father is; however, Hoffert believes that the passage in which Wheelwright ponders his religious beliefs and American politics are ''neither especially persuasive nor actively integrated into the book.''[13] Sybil Steinberg writes that *Owen Meany* is a ''contrived, preachy, tedious tale'' and that its ''meandering narrative'' is ''too 'mortally cute' for its own good.''[14] Although claiming that Irving is an ''abundantly and ever joyfully talented storyteller,'' Alfred Kazin says that the plot of *Owen Meany* is as ''discursive as an undergraduate bull session,'' that the novel ''does not translate convincingly as fiction,'' and that the book's main flaw is that there is ''no irony.''[15] After asking readers to recall the ''appalling family'' in *Hotel New Hampshire* and to wonder if the readers thought they were ''through'' with such characters, Peter S. Prescott warns: ''Here they come again, only slightly disguised, lurching out of whatever thicket Irving uses to refurbish his novels—like so many zombies from 'Night of the Living Dead.' . . . It will do no good to complain that this grossly long book lacks charm precisely because it works so hard to be sweet. Irving's fans, like hippopotami, will enjoy the wallow."[16]

Because he concentrated on wrestling while he was in college and was not "involved in the issue that really obsessed most American people [his] age—namely the draft and the war in Vietnam,"[17] this novel's subject matter is a logical progression in Irving's ficition since it was perhaps inevitable that he would analyze the Vietnam War's effects on and the lack of faith and religion in contemporary life. John Wheelwright's recollections mirror the chaos that results from a lack of faith in the government, politicians, movie stars, and God, all of which characterized the decade and made people unwitting victims during and after the Vietnam War. In this sense, Wheelwright's narrative is more portentous than the narrator's in *Marriage* and certainly less "cute" than John Berry's in *Hotel New Hampshire*.

In his earlier novels, Irving analyzes various contemporary issues: war, terrorism, rape, abortion, women's rights, mate swapping, and parental responsibility. In *Owen Meany*, he again analyzes a significant issue—the presence or absence of faith in God in the twentieth century. As with his other analyses, his examination of faith and miracles is troubling and thought provoking. At the same time, if his other novels are ultimately about living purposeful and meaningful lives despite life's forces, then *A Prayer for Owen Meany* is also about surviving despite what John Wheelwright calls the "condition of universal disappointment" (480). And in the world according to

Owen Meany, to survive universal disappointment requires prayers and faith, and says Owen, "FAITH TAKES PRACTICE."

NOTES

1. Richard Bernstein, "John Irving: 19th Century Novelist for These Times," C13.
2. John Irving, *A Prayer for Owen Meany*, 19; hereafter cited in the text.
3. Bernstein, "John Irving," C13.
4. Phyllis Robinson, "A Talk with John Irving," 3.
5. Michael Anderson, "Casting Doubt on Atheism," *New York Times Book Review*, March 12, 1989, 30.
6. R. Z. Sheppard, "Doing Things His Way," *Time* 133 (3 April 1989): 80.
7. Robinson, "A Talk with John Irving," 3.
8. *Ibid.*
9. R. Z. Sheppard, "The Message Is the Message," *Time*, 133 (3 April 1989): 80.
10. *Ibid.*
11. William Pritchard, "Small Town Saint," *The New Republic*, 200. 36 (22 May 1989): 37.
12. *Ibid.*, 38.
13. Barbara Hoffert, *Library Journal*, 113 (10 April 1989): 54.
14. Sybil Steinberg, "Forecasts," *Publishers Weekly*, 235 (6 January 1989): 89–90.
15. Alfred Kazin, "God's Own Little Squirt," *New York Times Book Review*, 12 March 1989, 30.
16. Peter S. Prescott, "Here They Come Again," *Newsweek*, 113 (10 April 1989): 64.
17. Larry McCaffery, "An Interview with John Irving," 5.

BIBLIOGRAPHY

Books

Setting Free the Bears. New York: Random House, 1968. London: Corgi Books, 1979.

The Water-Method Man. New York: Random House, 1972. London: Corgi Books, 1980.

The 158-Pound Marriage. New York: Random House, 1974. London: Corgi Books, 1980.

The World According to Garp. New York: E. P. Dutton, 1978. London: Victor Gollancz, 1978.

3 By Irving. New York: Random House, 1980. Comprises *Setting Free the Bears*, *The Water-Method Man*, and *The 158-Pound Marriage*.

The Hotel New Hampshire. New York: Dutton, 1981. London: Cape, 1981.

The Cider House Rules. New York: William Morrow, 1985. London: Cape, 1985.

A Prayer for Owen Meany. New York: William Morrow, 1989. London: Bloomsbury, 1989.

Short Stories

"A Winter Branch." *Redbook* 126 (November 1965): 56–57, 143–46.

"Weary Kingdom." *The Boston Review* (Spring–Summer 1968): 8–35.

"Lost in New York." *Esquire* 79 (March 1973): 116–17, 152.

''Almost in Iowa.'' *Esquire* 80 (November 1973): 143–46, 224–29.

''Brennbar's Rant.'' *Playboy* 21 (December 1974): 4, 137, 304–7.

''Students: These Are Your Teachers.'' *Esquire* 84 (September 1975): 68, 156–59.

''The Pension Grillparzer.'' *Antaeus* (Winter 1976): 7–27.

''Vigilance.'' *Ploughshares* 4 (1977): 103–14.

''Dog in the Alley, Child in the Sky.'' *Esquire* 87 (June 1977): 108–9, 158–62.

''Interior Space.'' *Fiction* 6 (1980): 26–58. (First written in 1974).

''A Bear Called State O'Maine.'' *Rolling Stone*, 20 August 1981, 22–27, 50–55. (Excerpt from *Hotel New Hampshire*).

''The Foul Ball.'' *New Yorker*, 64 (30 January 1988): 28–40, 44–46, 50–52, 54–56. (Excerpt with variations from *Owen Meany*).

''The Making of a Writer: Trying to Save Piggy Snead.'' *New York Times Book Review*, 22 August 1982, 3, 20–22. Reprinted in *The Breadloaf Anthology of Contemporary American Short Stories*, edited by Robert Pack and Jay Parini, 155–68. Breadloaf, Vt.: University Press of New England, 1987.

Poetry

''For Fitch Retired.'' *Year of the Dog*. Putney, Vt.: The Year of the Dog, 1972.

Selected Essays and Nonfiction

''Gorgeous Dan.'' *Esquire* 79 (April 1973): 106–9, 217–21.

''Neglected Books of the Twentieth Century.'' *Antaeus* 27 (Autumn 1977): 131–32.

''Life After Graduation According to Garp.'' *Esquire* 91 (27 March 1979): 53.

''Best Seller: What Does It Really Mean?'' *Vogue* 169 (April 1969): 154, 156.

''Works in Progress.'' *New York Times Book Review*, 15 July 1979, 1, 14. Comments about *Hotel New Hampshire*.

''Kurt Vonnegut and His Critics: The Aesthetics of Accessibility.'' *New Republic* 181 (22 September 1979): 41–42.

"In Defense of Sentimentality." *New York Times Book Review*, 25 November 1979, 3, 96.

"TABA Winners: No Thanks and Thanks." *New York Times Book Review*, 25 May 1980, 3–4, 14–15.

"Obnoxious." *New York Times Book Review*, 19 September 1982, 35. Letter to the editor in response to Harold Brodkey's "My Most Obnoxious Writer," *New York Times Book Review*, 29 August 1982, Sec. 1, 7.

"The Narrative Voice." In *Voicelust: Eight Contemporary Fiction Writers on Style*, edited by Allen Wier and Don Hendrie Jr., 87–92. Lincoln: University of Nebraska Press, 1985.

Selected Book Reviews

"Facts of Living." Review of *The Stories of John Cheever*, by John Cheever. *Saturday Review* 5 (30 September 1978): 44–46.

"An Expose of Heaven and Hell." Review of *The Living End*, by Stanley Elkin. *New York Times Book Review*, 10 June 1979, 7, 30.

"Father and Son." Review of *The Duke of Deception*, by Geoffrey Wolff. *New York Times Book Review*, 12 August 1979, 1, 18, 20.

"Stories with Voiceprints." Review of *Black Tickets*, by Jayne Anne Phillips. *New York Times Book Review*, 30 September 1979, 13, 28.

"Morrison's Fable." Review of *Tar Baby*, by Toni Morrison. *New York Times Book Review*, 29 March 1981, 1, 30–31.

"Günter Grass: King of the Toy Merchants." Review of *Headbirths, or The Germans are Dying Out*, by Günter Grass. *Saturday Review* 9 (March 1982): 57–60.

"Risking All for Gold and Grizzlies." Review of *Seven Rivers West*, by Edward Hoagland. *New York Times Book Review*, 21 September 1986, 1, 44–45.

Interviews

Anderson, Michael. "Casting Doubts on Atheism." *New York Times Book Review*, 12 March 1989, 30. Irving comments on religious faith in his life and in *Owen Meany*.

Bannon, Barbara. "*PW* Interviews John Irving." *Publishers Weekly* 213 (24 April 1978): 6–7. Contains biographical information and comments by Irving.

Bernstein, Richard. "John Irving: 19th Century Novelist For These Times." *New York Times*, 25 April 1989, C13, C17. Irving comments on *Owen Meany*, its narrator, and religious ideas.

Bonnetti, Kay. "An Interview with John Irving." Columbia, Mo.: American Audio Prose Library, 1979. Audio Cassette. Irving comments on his life, writings, and techniques.

de Coppet, Laura. "An Interview with John Irving." *Interview* 11 (October 1981): 42–44. Irving discusses bear symbolism, literary beliefs, *Garp*, and *Hotel New Hampshire*. This interview appeared in condensed form in *Book-of-the-Month-Club News* (November 1981): 4–5.

Feron, James. "All About Writing, According to Irving." *New York Times*, 29 November 1981, Sec. 22, 4. Irving provides insights into his techniques and works.

Hansen, Ron. "The Art of Fiction XCIII: John Irving." *Paris Review* 28. 100 (1986): 74–103. Irving talks about his favorite writers, literary theory, and works.

Kummer, Corby. "John Irving: Fascinated by Orphans." *Book-of-the-Month-Club News* (Summer 1985): 5. Kummer provides new insights into Irving's life, especially about his natural father.

McCaffery, Larry. "An Interview with John Irving." *Contemporary Literature* 23 (Winter 1982): 1–18. Irving discusses his novels, favorite writers, and his ideas about fiction.

Priestly, Michael. "An Interview with John Irving." *New England Review* (Summer 1979): 489–504. As an early interview, it contains interesting insights into Irving's novels and literary beliefs.

Renwick, Joyce. "John Irving: An Interview." *Fiction International* 14 (1982): 5–18. Irving comments about his wrestling metaphors, his novels, and literary techniques.

Robinson, Phyllis. "A Talk With John Irving." *Book-of-the-Month-Club News* (April 1989): 3. Irving talks about religious faith in *Owen Meany*.

Sanoff, Alvin P. "A Conversation With John Irving: 'Humans Are a Violent Species—We Always Have Been.' " *U.S. News & World Report* 91 (26 October 1981): 70–71. Irving talks about violence in American life.

West, Richard. "John Irving's World After *Garp*." *New York Magazine* 14 (17 August 1981): 29–32. Irving discusses *Garp*, *Hotel New Hampshire*, *Cider House*, and violence in his works.

Williams, Thomas. "Talk with John Irving." *New York Times Book Review*, 23 April 1978, 6.

Critical Studies

BIBLIOGRAPHY

Reilly, Edward C. "A John Irving Bibliography." *Bulletin of Bibliography* 42 (March 1985): 12–18. Primary and secondary materials are included.

BOOKS

Harter, Carol C., and James R. Thompson. *John Irving*. Boston: Twayne, 1986. A comprehensive study of Irving's career and his novels from *Setting Free the Bears* to *The Cider House Rules*.

Miller, Gabriel. *John Irving*. New York: Frederick Ungar, 1982. This first book-length study discusses Irving's life and novels from *Bears* to *Hotel New Hampshire*.

BIOGRAPHICAL SOURCES

Haller, Scott. "John Irving's Bizarre World." *Saturday Review* 9 (September 1981): 30–32, 34. Facts about Irving's life are supplemented with Irving's comments.

Land, Irene Stokvis. "First Novelists." *Library Journal* 93 (1 October 1968): 3587–88. Irving relates biographical information.

Moritz, Charles, ed. *Current Biography Yearbook 1979*, 178–81. New York: H. W. Wilson, 1979. Useful biographical facts make this source valuable for all Irving readers.

Ruppersburg, Hugh M. "John Irving." In *Dictionary of Literary Biography: American Novelists Since World War II*, Second Series, edited by James E. Kibler Jr., 153–61. Detroit: Bruccoli Clark/Gale Research, 1980. Provides comprehensive biographical information and critical ideas.

Sheppard, R. Z. "Life Into Art: Garp Creator Strikes Again." *Time* 118 (31 August 1981): 46–51. There are comments by Irving, his mother, friends, and other contemporary writers.

SELECTED CRITICISM

Budd, John. "The Inadequacy of Brevity: John Irving's Short Fiction." *The Round Table* 26 (Spring 1985): 4–6. Discusses "Lost in New York" and "Almost in Iowa," which contain characters, conflicts, and themes similar to those in the novels.

Carton, Evan. "The Politics of Selfhood: Bob Slocum, T. S. Garp, and Auto-American-Biography." *The Novel: A Forum on Fiction* 20 (Fall 1986): 46–61. Carton argues that while similar in their central characters and images of social reality, Irving's *Garp* is reactionary in depicting selfhood and politics, but Heller's *Something Happened* is revisionary.

Cosgrove, William. "*The World According to Garp* as Fabulation." *South Carolina Review* 19 (Spring 1987): 52–58. *Garp* contains the elements of fabulation as were typical in the eighteenth- and nineteenth-century novels: ironies, implausibilities, a plot developed through dramatic incidents, and an omniscent narrator.

DeMott, Benjamin. "Guilt and Compassion." *New York Times Book Review*, 26 May 1985, 1, 25. DeMott provides interesting insights into and criticism of *The Cider House Rules*.

Dickstein, Morris. "The World As Mirror." *Sewanee Review* 89 (Summer 1981): 386–400. Dickstein uses Styron's *Sophie's Choice*, Roth's *The Ghost Writer*, Malamud's *Dubin's Lives*, and Irving's *Garp* to prove that writers create "autobiographical protagonists" who mirror the author's experiences; that one novel reads like the others; and that they are "confessional but confess little."

Doane, Janice, and Devon Hodges. *Nostalgia and Sexual Difference*. New York: Meuthen, 1987. See especially "Women and *The World According to Garp*," 65–76, which argues that the novel's plot actually supports male and paternal authority.

Drabble, Margaret. "Muck, Memory, and Imagination," *Harper's* 257 (July 1978): 82–84. A seminal review with insights into *Garp*, its themes and esthetics.

Gilbert, Susan. "Children of the 70s: The American Family in Recent Fiction." *Soundings* 63 (Summer 1980): 199–213. In discussing Cheever's *Falconer*, Stegner's *The Spectator Bird*, Didion's *The Book of Common Prayer*, and Irving's *Garp*, Gilbert concludes that the American family is rootless, that the family unit cannot protect itself from pain, and that these novels plead for some cohesive unity.

Hill, Jane Bowers. "John Irving's Aesthetics of Accessibility: Setting

Free the Novel." *South Carolina Review* 16 (Fall 1983): 38–44. Hill uses Irving's essay, "Kurt Vonnegut and His Critics," to discuss Irving as a serious, major, and accessible writer.

Lounsberry, Barbara. "The Terrible Under Toad: Violence as Excessive Imagination in *The World According to Garp*." *Thalia* 5 (Fall-Winter 1982–1983): 30–35. Lounsberry argues that extremes of imagination in regards to sex, sexual politics, child rearing, and literature exacerbate extremism, often with violent results.

Marcus, Greil. "John Irving: The World of *The World According to Garp*." *Rolling Stone*, 13 December 1979, 68–75. A seminal article with comments by Irving about rape and violence.

———. "Garp: Death in the Family, I." *Rolling Stone*, 24 August 1978, 60, 62. "Garp: Death in the Family, II." *Rolling Stone*, 21 September 1978, 76, 79. Greil provides interesting insights into *Garp* and its major themes.

Nelson, William. "The Comic Grotesque in Recent Fiction." *Thalia* 5 (Fall–Winter 1982–1983): 36–40. Nelson uses Toole's *A Confederacy of Dunces*, Robbins's *Even Cowgirls Get the Blues*, and Irving's *Garp* to discuss the comic grotesque characters and their courses of action.

Priestly, Michael. "Structure in the Worlds of John Irving." *Critique* 23 (1981): 82–96. While imposing a personal order on the novels' worlds in his first four novels, Irving's own plots question such an order's tenability since the characters independently search for their own order and meaning in life.

Reilly, Edward C. "The *Anschluss* and the World According to Irving." *Research Studies* 51 (June 1983): 98–110. As a major metaphor, the *Anschluss* colors the conflicts and violence in *Setting Free the Bears*, *Garp*, and *Hotel New Hampshire*.

———. "A Note About Two Toads." *Notes on Contemporary Literature* 14 (May 1984): 7–8. Toad symbolism in *Garp* and D. H. Lawrence's *The Virgin and the Gypsy*.

———. "John Irving's *The Hotel New Hampshire* and the Allegory of Sorrow." *Publications of the Arkansas Philological Association* 9 (Spring 1983): 78–83. The Berry's Labrador retriever, aptly named Sorrow, symbolizes life's overwhelming forces.

———. "Life Into Art: Some Notes on Irving's Fiction." *Notes on Contemporary Literature* 13 (September 1983): 8–9. Irving translates incidents from his own life into the magic of fiction.

Thompson, Christine E. "Pentheus in *The World According to Garp*." *Classical and Modern Literature* 3 (Fall 1982); 33–37. Thompson discusses the Pentheus myth as it relates to the feminist funeral sequence in *Garp*.

Walker, Nancy. "John Irving." In *Critical Survey of Long Fiction, Vol. IV*, edited by Frank N. Magill, 1413–25. LaCanada, Cal.: Salem Press, 1983. Walker provides biographical information and critical insights into Irving's first five novels.

Wymard, Eleanor B. "New Visions of the Midas Touch: *Daniel Martin* and *The World According to Garp*." *Modern Fiction Studies* 27 (Summer 1981): 284–86. Wymard compares the two works and their authors who affirm and accept the joys and trials of "everyday living."

Index

Anschluss, 3, 4, 16, 18, 19, 21, 22, 23, 29, 47, 48, 49, 51, 61, 63, 69, 81–84, 94, 101, 122, 136

Cheever, John, 5
Conrad, Joseph, 10

Dickens, Charles, 5, 10, 78, 117
Dostoevsky, Fyodor, 10

Ford, Ford Madox: *The Good Soldier,* 47, 60, 60 n.1

Ginsberg, Harvey, 118
Grass, Günter, 15, 78, 141

Hardy, Thomas, 10
Hawkes, John, 10, 47, 60, 60 n.1

Irving, Brendan, 2
Irving, Colin, 2
Irving, Colin F.N., 1
Irving, John: affirmative endings, 7, 8–9, 33; autobiography and fiction, 2–3, 11, 143; bildungsroman, 6–7; comedy/tragedy juxtaposition, 7–8; epilogues, 10–11; fictional heros/heroines, 6, 7, 21, 50, 61, 64, 68, 128; literary techniques, 42, 71, 76, 81, 101, 103, 104, 110, 121, 124; metaphors, 9; plots, 10–11; refrains, 8–9; settings 3–5; symbolism, 9–19, 93

Characters:

Bates, Iowa Bob (*Hotel*), 88, 89, 90, 91, 92, 95, 97

Bears: Asiatic Black Bear (*Bears*), 25–26, 70; Duna the Circus Bear (Garp), 70; Rare Spectacled (*Bears*), 26–27, 70; State O'Maine (''Earl'' *Hotel*), 82, 93–94, 98; Susie the Bear (*Hotel*), 84, 93, 94–95, 98, 129
Bender, George James (*Marriage*), 53, 56
Bennett, Cuthbert (''Cuth'') (*Water-Method*), 39–40, 41, 42
Benno Blum Gang (*Bears, Marriage*), 18, 48, 55
Berry, Egg (*Hotel*), 87, 89, 90, 91, 97
Berry, Frank (*Hotel*), 84, 86–87, 89, 90, 91, 97
Berry, Franny (*Hotel*), 84, 85–86, 89, 92, 93, 95, 97, 98
Berry, John (*Hotel*), 9, 50, 81, 82, 83, 85–86, 89–90, 94, 95, 143
Berry, Lilly (*Hotel*), 84, 87, 91, 94, 98
Berry, Mary Bates (''Mother'') (*Hotel*), 7, 82, 87, 89, 91, 92, 97
Berry, Winslow, (''Father'') (*Hotel*), 82, 84, 89, 91, 92, 93
Bowlsby, Florence Cocharan (''Mrs. Ralph'') (*Garp*), 76
Cannon, Audrey (*Marriage*), 50, 52, 53, 57
Dove, Chipper (*Hotel*), 85, 88, 98
Duna. *See* Bears
Eames, Miss (*Cider House*), 104, 109, 112
Eames, Mrs. (*Cider House*), 104, 109, 112
Eastman, Alfred (*Owen Meany*), 139
Eastman, Hester (*Owen Meany*), 123, 125, 127, 129–32, 139
Eastman, Martha (*Owen Meany*), 139
Ellen Jamesians, 66, 67, 74. *See also* James, Ellen
Fields, Jenny (*Garp*), 63, 65–67, 68, 69, 72, 76
Fletcher, Harrison and Alice (Garp), 63, 64
Freud (*Hotel*), 83, 87–88, 91, 93, 98
Garp, Duncan (*Garp*), 63, 64, 67, 70, 74–75
Garp, Jenny (*Garp*), 70, 72, 76
Garp, Walt (*Garp*), 48, 63, 64, 68, 74, 77
Garp, T. S. (*Garp*), 3–4, 6–7, 9, 36, 54, 63–65, 76, 77, 84
Glanz, Zahn (*Bears*), 16, 27–28, 49
Graff, Hames (*Bears*), 6, 15, 16, 19, 21–23, 25–26, 29, 30
Hellein, Anna (*Bears*), 18
Holm, Ernie (*Garp*), 63, 64, 72, 74
Holm, Helen (*Garp*), 64, 65, 68, 71, 75, 77, 105
James, Ellen (*Garp*), 63, 66, 69, 76. *See also* Ellen Jamesians
Jarvits, Dick (*Owen Meany*), 137, 140
Jarvits, Frank (*Owen Meany*), 136–37
Javotnik, Siegfried (''Siggy'') (*Bears*), 6, 15, 16, 17, 18, 19, 20–25 passim, 29, 64
Javotnik, Vratno (*Bears*), 23, 24, 25

Kendall, Ray (*Cider House*), 102, 107, 109, 114, 115
Kendle, Lydia (*Water-Method*), 36, 37
Knezevich, Zivan (*Marriage*), 50, 52, 55
Kudashvili, Captain (*Marriage*), 51, 55
Kunft, Sue ("Biggie") (*Water-Method*), 33, 36, 40–41, 44
Larch, Wilbur (*Cider House*), 8, 102, 103, 104–5, 108, 109, 111, 112–13, 114, 115, 125
Marek, Katrina (*Bears, Marriage*), 49, 50, 55
Marter, Grandfather (*Bears*), 21, 23, 24, 27
Marter, Grandmother (*Bears*), 18, 21, 23, 25
Marter, Hilke (*Bears*), 16, 21, 23
Meany, Mr. (*Owen Meany*), 138
Meany, Mrs. (*Owen Meany*), 132, 135, 136
Meany, Owen (*Owen Meany*), 6, 9, 121–22, 123–26 passim, 127, 130–134 passim, 137, 139–40, 142, 143–44
Melony (*Cider House*), 107–8, 109, 114, 115, 129
Merrill, Reverand Lewis (*Owen Meany*), 129, 132, 134–35
Mihailovich, Colonel Drazha (*Bears*), 19, 20, 24, 25
Milton, Michael (*Garp*), 65, 71, 77
Muldoon, Roberta (*Garp*), 67–68, 77
Needham, Dan (*Owen Meany*), 122, 123, 127, 129, 133–34, 135, 139, 140
Neff, Drexa (*Bears, Marriage*), 27, 49, 55
Overturf, Merrill (*Water-Method*), 34, 35, 38–39, 40, 42
Rawls, Major (*Owen Meany*), 136, 137
Rose, Mr. (*Cider House*), 109, 113, 115
Rose, Rose (*Cider House*), 106, 109, 111, 113, 115
Schuschnigg, Chancellor Kurt Von (*Bears*), 18, 26, 28
Slivinca, Bijelo (*Bears*), 20, 28
Slivinca, Todor (*Bears*), 23, 24, 28
Sorrow (*Hotel*), 89–91, 97, 98, 116
State O'Maine. *See* Bears
Susie the Bear. *See* Bears
Thalhammer, Anna Agati. *See* Utchka
Trianovich, Vaso (*Marriage*), 50, 52, 55
Trumper, Colm (*Water-Method*), 35, 38, 40, 41, 42
Trumper, Fred "Bogus" (*Water-Method*), 6, 33, 34, 37–38, 40–42, 44, 45, 64, 84
Tulpen (*Water-Method*), 37, 38, 39, 40, 41, 42, 43
Under Toad, The (*Garp*), 10, 73–75, 89, 116
Utchka ("Utch") (*Marriage*), 6, 7, 41, 47, 49, 50, 51–52, 53, 54
Watzek-Trummer, Ernst (*Bears*), 23, 27, 29

Wells, Angel (*Cider House*), 106, 108, 112, 114, 116
Wells, Homer (*Cider House*), 3, 6, 7, 101, 103, 104–5, 106–9 passim, 111, 112–13, 114, 115, 125
Wheelwright, John (*Owen Meany*), 3, 5, 6, 50, 121–22, 124–27, 130–34 passim, 137, 139–43 passim
Wheelwright, Tabitha ("Tabby") (*Owen Meany*), 7, 125, 132, 133, 135
Winter, Edith (*Marriage*), 51, 52, 53, 54, 57–58
Winter, Severin (*Marriage*), 49, 50, 52–53, 54, 56, 57–58, 67, 84
Worthington, Olive (*Cider House*), 108, 109
Worthington, Wallace Sr. (*Cider House*), 108
Worthington, Wally (*Cider House*), 4, 101–2, 103, 106–8 passim, 111–14 passim, 116
Wut, Gottlob (*Bears*), 19, 21, 23, 24

Works:

Cider House Rules, The, 2–4, 8, 9, 12, 24, 41, 46, 70, 99, 101–19, 121, 125, 141; affirmative ending, 115–16; bildungsroman, 105, 106, 107; critical reception, 118–19; metaphors, 111–14; refrains, 114–15; themes, 110–11
Hotel New Hampshire, The, 2, 4, 5, 8, 9, 10, 12, 24, 25, 33, 41, 46, 70, 73, 79, 81–99, 118, 119, 129, 139, 142, 143; affirmative ending, 95–96; bear symbolism, 93–95, 98–99; bildungsroman, 85, 92; critical reception, 96–97; refrains, 90–92; sports metaphor (weight lifting), 88–89; symbolism, 92, 93, 98
158-Pound Marriage, The, 2, 3, 4, 6, 8, 33, 41, 46, 47–60, 62, 63, 64, 67, 68, 69, 73, 76, 77, 97, 143; affirmative ending, 59; critical reception, 59–60; refrain, 58–59; sports metaphor (wrestling), 56–58
Prayer for Owen Meany, A, 2, 4, 8, 9, 12, 119, 121–44, affirmative ending, 143; ciritical reception, 141–43; family themes, 137–39; sports metaphor (slam-dunking), 139–40; symbolism, 140–41
Setting Free the Bears, 2, 3, 5, 8, 9, 10, 15–31, 33, 36, 41, 43, 47, 48, 49, 59, 62, 68, 69, 73, 76, 77, 79, 93, 97; affirmative ending, 29–30; comedy/tragedy juxtaposition, 27–28; critical reception, 30; refrains, 24–25; symbolism, 25–27; themes, 22–24
Water-Method Man, The, 2, 4, 6, 8, 9, 12, 33–46, 56, 59, 60, 63, 68, 74, 76, 77, 97; affirmative ending, 44–45; comedy, 34–36, 37; critical reception, 45–46; refrains, 42–43
World According to Garp, The, 2, 3, 4, 5, 6, 7, 8, 10, 24, 25, 33, 36, 41, 43, 44, 46, 60, 61–80, 91, 93, 95, 96, 105, 117, 118, 119, 134; affirmative ending, 75–76; critical reception, 77–79; rape, 69–70, 71; sports metaphor (wrestling), 72–73

Index

Kesey, Ken, 21
Kershner, Irwin, 2

Leary, Shyla, 2

Madoff, Mara, 17, 18, 19

Robbins, Henry, 77, 118

Tolstoi, Leo, 10
Turgenev, Ivan, 10
Turnbull, Janet, 2

Vienna, Austria, 2, 3, 4, 5, 11, 15, 18, 19, 22, 34–35, 42, 48, 49, 59, 61–63, 79, 81–82, 92–93, 98, 122
Vonnegut, Kurt, 5, 12

Woolf, Virginia, 10